POLITICAL COMMUNICATION STRATEGIES IN
POST-INDEPENDENCE JAMAICA, 1972–2006

POLITICAL COMMUNICATION STRATEGIES IN POST-INDEPENDENCE JAMAICA, 1972–2006

Floyd E. Morris

The University of the West Indies Press

Jamaica • Barbados • Trinidad and Tobago

The University of the West Indies Press
7A Gibraltar Hall Road, Mona
Kingston 7, Jamaica
www.uwipress.com

A catalogue record of this book is available from the National Library
of Jamaica.

ISBN: 978-976-640-780-3 (paper)
978-976-640-781-0 (Kindle)
978-976-640-782-7 (ePub)

Cover design by Vennessa Hanshaw

Printed in the United States of America

This book is dedicated to three people who have had a magnanimous impact on my life. First, my mother, Miss Jemita Pryce, who instilled discipline and the value of education. Second, the Honourable Horace Clarke, a former member of Parliament for Central St Mary and minister of government and now deceased, who gave tremendous support during the period I became blind and also assisted with my tertiary education. Third, Noel Gayle, the father of my beautiful and supportive wife, who gave me tremendous encouragement to complete my Doctor of Philosophy, and while he too is deceased, his fatherly support is hereby acknowledged.

Contents

Acknowledgements

The writing of a book is a challenging academic undertaking. Along the journey, there are individuals who served in various capacities to get the work done. I wish to express my profound appreciation to these individuals for their tireless support. I also wish to thank my God and church community for the love, encouragement and support given during the process of this research.

I wish to express sincere appreciation to the subjects under study in this book: Michael Manley, Edward Seaga and P.J. Patterson, for the insights given relating to their work and leadership of Jamaica. Furthermore, to all those who participated in the elite interviews, I am forever grateful. Their insights formed the core of the deliberation in this book, and I am eternally grateful to them.

To those who gave me overwhelming research support, especially Chevelle Gerson, Glenise Henry and Ashley Codner, I am extremely grateful. Also, to my wife, Shelley-Ann, I owe more than a debt of gratitude, for it is her tolerance, patience and understanding that allowed me to complete this work.

I wish to also express profound gratitude to Neville "Struggle" Martin, author of the song "The Message", for giving me permission to use the content of his music in my book. His work is hereby acknowledged.

Finally, I must express tremendous gratitude to Professor Hopeton Dunn for the exceptional guidance he has given me for this book. The completion of this book is inextricably linked to his depth of knowledge and intellectual fortitude. His sage counsel and guidance have assisted in shaping in me a greater understanding of political communication in Jamaica.

Abbreviations

CARICOM	Caribbean Community
CCJ	Caribbean Court of Justice
CDMA	code-division multiple access
CSM	Caribbean Single Market
CSME	CARICOM Single Market and Economy
ECJ	Electoral Commission of Jamaica
FINSAC	Financial Sector Adjustment Company
GATT	General Agreement on Tariffs and Trade
HEART	Human Employment and Resource Training
IMF	International Monetary Fund
JAMAL	Jamaica Movement for the Advancement of Literacy
JBC	Jamaica Broadcasting Corporation
JIS	Jamaica Information Service
JLP	Jamaica Labour Party
NAM	Non-Aligned Movement
NDM	National Democratic Movement
NEC	National Executive Council
NIEO	New International Economic Order
NIR	net international reserves
NWICO	New Information and Communication Order
NYS	National Youth Service
PATH	Programme of Advancement through Health and Education
PNP	People's National Party
PRIDE	Programme for Resettlement and Integrated Development Enterprise
RJR	Radio Jamaica and Rediffusion
ROSE	Re-organisation of Secondary Education
STATIN	Statistical Institute of Jamaica
UNDP	United Nations Development Programme
USSR	Union of Soviet Socialist Republics
WTO	World Trade Organization

Introduction

For democracy to thrive in any society, there must be effective communication. In a liberal democratic society, leaders and their political parties take on the responsibility of representing the people. In this process, they formulate programmes and policies to foster development, and put mechanisms in place to accommodate communication and receive feedback.

In approaches to politics, citizens have become more like consumers (instrumental, oriented to immediate gratification, and potentially fickle) than believers, and as Blumler and Kavanagh (1999) note, politicians must work harder to retain their interest and support. This reflects the challenges and realities that confront contemporary political communication. It highlights the issues affecting citizens' participation or nonparticipation in the liberal democratic process and the need for politicians to find new ways of engaging with them.

An interesting and intriguing discipline, political science embraces other subdisciplines such as international relations, public administration, political philosophy and, more recently, political communication. Even though it is a recent development, earlier political actors found ways and means of communicating with their audience centuries ago. Political communication incorporates the various modalities of the communication process and is the continuous transference of political information between stakeholders within the public sphere (Norris 2004).

In the context of liberal democracy, the subject of political communication has involved a dialogue on freedom versus order. *Freedom*, in this context, refers to basic civil liberties, while *order* refers to the levels of restriction that exist within a society (Hahn 2003). The debate has seen the evolution of two distinct groups, categorized as "liberals" and "conservatives". Liberals believe that to facilitate meaningful development, the freedom of individuals must be given prominence and be respected. Conversely, conservatives believe that to facilitate the development of civilization and preserve the freedom of individuals, order must be maintained.

Political Communication and Media

It must be noted that while both groups believe in order and freedom, the distinction lies in the priority that each group gives to the issues that arise from the dialogue. Liberals believe that freedom comes first, while conservatives believe that order is the fundamental priority (Hahn 2003). The critical point of intersection and equilibrium comes at freedom of expression, freedom of assembly and property rights. Both groups believe that these elements are fundamental to the preservation of democracy and ultimately enhance the practice of political communication (Habermas 2006).

The dialectics on freedom and order have intensified over the years through varied social institutions. Habermas (1989) described them as the public sphere where the dialogue manifests itself in conversations on a wide variety of issues. An active participant in the dialogue is the media (Dahlgren 2000a). The development of the media over the years has given new impetus to this area of political communication.

In Jamaica, political leaders have adopted multiple strategies to communicate with and inspire people to national action. Some of them have worked successfully, while others have failed miserably. It is posited that ineffective communication has contributed to voter apathy, and ultimately to the failure of some leaders. Prior to this, this belief was not examined; therefore, this work generates new knowledge and adds to the existing literature in the field of political communication.

It must be noted that this author is not suggesting that ineffective communication is the sole cause of political apathy. Factors such as corruption, poor governance, unfulfilled expectations, disillusionment, arrogance and mismanagement have contributed to political apathy in Jamaica and the broader Caribbean (Waller 2013; Munroe 2002; Stone 1989a, 1989b). However, the focus of this book is on political communication.

There has been a radical change in the political landscape of Jamaica, largely due to the transformation that has taken place in the media. Prior to the 1940s, television stations in Jamaica were nonexistent, and the Internet was unknown. The development of satellite technology and invention of the transmitter facilitated a radical change in the way that political actors have communicated to their audiences since the 1970s. The political landscape virtually became a theatre, as the ability of leaders to speak, act and charm merged with the possibilities presented by audiotape and camera; the result was an intensification of competition between political organizations as they tried to win the minds and hearts of their constituents (Graber 2011).

Due to the significant growth of the media in Jamaica since 1980 and its liberalization in 1991, citizens are now more exposed to diverse varieties and formats of information as new players have been introduced to the industry. By 2012, there were three major national newspapers, three free-to-air television stations, twenty-seven radio stations broadcasting nationally and forty-one cable providers (Dunn 2012). The Internet also became a major part of the landscape as citizens were able to use diverse social media platforms to articulate their views on national issues. This massive expansion assisted in exposing the dialectic taking place in the public sphere and exposed the failure of politicians to advance the levels of development needed to empower the people. Consequently, conflicts emerged and politicians were seen as strong on rhetoric and weak on deliverables (Blumler and Gurevitch 2001). Despite global developments, however, political parties in Jamaica and the wider English-speaking Caribbean have been lagging. Apparently, they lack the necessary structural reforms to address the dwindling support for their organizations.

The level of political competition intensified as liberal democracy (Munroe 2002) throughout the world took on a new shape and form. In this regard, the media played a pivotal role, as its rapid expansion exposed more people to a new political culture (Blumler and Kavanagh 1999). By the latter part of the twentieth century, the political theatre of Jamaica entered homes via cable, satellite and the Internet. This resulted in an informed citizenry, now empowered to make rational choices. As globalization (Giddens 1991) took root and liberalization (Munroe 2002) became in vogue, more and more individuals focused on themselves instead of on traditional organizations, resulting in less time and effort spent with grassroot organizations such as political parties. This had profound implications for the advancement of liberal democracy (Giddens 1991).

The intensification of the process of Americanization and cultural penetration facilitated by the media also prompted a virtually new political culture throughout the world. Globally, voters were becoming more aware and more independent of traditional social and political institutions such as political parties (Hallin and Mancini 2004). A decline in voter participation and support for political parties was reflected in Europe and North America, where recent elections showed that less than 50 per cent of the electorate participated in national polls (Friedman 2012). In Jamaica and the rest of the English-speaking Caribbean, a similar situation was occurring.

After winning an election and assuming the mantle of government, political leaders are confronted with certain economic realities. This may affect their ability to keep their campaign promises. Politicians who fail to communicate these challenges add to citizens' frustration, causing a major trust deficit. Consequently, political leaders are now required to apply modern political approaches to regain the trust and confidence of constituents in order to re-engage them in the voting process. The use of modern, innovative political communication strategies is a cogent response, and failure to design them could mean facing public disorder and ridicule. This process, however, must be driven by empirical data so that it can withstand academic and professional scrutiny.

The approach to political communication forms the core premise of this book. This growth in the Jamaican media landscape correlates with simultaneous growth in the levels of uncommitted voters in the country. Statistics indicate that over 40 per cent of the voting population is ambivalent about the political process (Anderson 2015). The fundamental question concerns what is contributing to this growing ambivalence among voters. Feedback seems to indicate that one of the reasons is a serious deficit in the way that leaders communicate programmes and policies to citizens. It is for these reasons that this book was written.

This is the first book of its kind in Jamaica, and it will contribute to a greater understanding of political communication, political culture and the broader political landscape. Central to this understanding are the arguments of D.F. Hahn, Jürgen Habermas, Carl Stone, Harold Lasswell, Stuart Hall, Marshall McLuhan and others who have developed theories that give insights into the subject of political communication.

Media and Leadership in Jamaica

In Jamaica, the Internet has become a significant part of the landscape, giving rise to a plethora of social media sites such as Facebook and Twitter. The result has been a demand for better performance from political leaders because of this enhanced access to information. Voters have become more independent and individualistic, and therefore less willing to support the collectivism of political parties. Public opinion polls show over 40 per cent of the voting population as apathetic and uninterested in participating in the electoral process (Anderson 2015). Programmes and policies articulated during election campaigns are often not fully implemented, which has contributed to growing frustration among citizens (Graber 2011).

Since gaining independence from Britain in the early 1960s, Jamaicans have been exposed to several interesting political leaders. Their means of communicating programmes and policies to citizens have often been quite captivating. Edward Seaga, prime minister from 1980 to 1989, developed a skill for using the local vernacular and patois in his speeches, such as "light a candle, sing a Sankey and find your way back home" (*Jamaica Observer*, 13 December 2015). This was also done by Alexander Bustamante, who served as prime minister from 1962 to 1967. In one of his famous statements, Bustamante said, "Shoot me first, before you shoot my people" (Jones 2009). The uniqueness of this approach to communication by some Jamaican leaders has elicited different responses and results from the voting population.

In Jamaica and the wider English-speaking Caribbean, limited scientific studies have been conducted to determine the efficacy of communication strategies used by political leaders to communicate with citizens. While extensive work has been done on the political process and political system, research on the way that decisions are taken by government and transmitted to citizens, as well as the mechanisms in place for providing input and feedback, is nonexistent. In sum, there is very limited research that has been done on the development of mediated political communication (Hill and Hughes 1997) in modern Jamaica (that is, in the last forty years). An examination of the holdings of the West Indies and Special Collections at the Main Library on the Mona campus of the University of the West Indies revealed only two major studies completed in this area: "The Press and the 1967 General Election in Jamaica", by Kenneth Chin-Inn, and "Politics, Ideology and the Media in Jamaica: An Analysis of the Development of the Electronic Media, 1972–1992", by Bernard Jankee. Accordingly, there are ample research opportunities to fill the lacuna in this aspect of Caribbean political life.

Objectives

The success or failure of a political leader and administration in modern Jamaica is closely linked to an effective communication strategy for programmes and policies. In this context, leaders' understanding of the nature of the dialectics taking place in the public sphere, particularly the media, is important. The level of understanding and the nature of the responses to these discourses will assist in determining their success or failure. Thus, within the framework of liberal democracy and political communication, the ultimate indicator of political success or failure is regarded as the winning or losing of an election, as this is the forum where the population approves or disapproves of proposed programmes and policies.

This book, therefore, analyses mediated political communication (Hill and Hughes 1997) in modern Jamaica during the period 1972–2006 by determining:

- How communication strategies of selected political leaders have served to engage citizen participation during this period
- The nature of the relationship between political leaders and citizens in mass mobilization in Jamaica
- The effects of the media representation of political masses on group membership and political party involvement in Jamaica

In considering these issues, the following questions are raised: What communication methods and techniques have been deployed in the exercise of power in relation to the perceived popular source of that power – the people? What is the relationship among leaders leading individuals and the wider society they seek to influence? How is change effected or stymied by political communication?

In addition to articulating a strategic political communication methodology that is applicable and relevant to the region, the book formulates an approach towards communicating programmes and policies of government to the people. It must be noted that most countries in the English-speaking Caribbean are postcolonial territories modelled on the Westminster system. As a result, there is a great deal of homogeneity, which makes it possible for the arguments made here to be applicable in this geographical space.

This volume presents a comparative analysis of the political communication strategies of three of Jamaica's political leaders during the period 1972 to 2006 – the liberalization period of the media landscape. Prime ministers Michael Manley, Edward Seaga and P.J. Patterson hailed from the country's two prominent political parties, the People's National Party (PNP) and the Jamaica Labour Party (JLP), and had distinct leadership characteristics. They were also the only leaders who served two or more full terms since Jamaica gained its political independence from Britain in 1962 (regarded as the modern era of Jamaican politics) and were considered significant achievers.

Michael Manley was tall, handsome and articulate; he served as prime minister from 1972 to 1980, and again from 1989 to 1992. He was known for using his charisma to persuade the masses to buy into his PNP government's programmes and policies (Panton 1993). Manley was the first Jamaican politician to be re-elected in two distinctly different political times: the Cold War and post–Cold War eras.

Patterson served from 1992 to 2006. He was portrayed as a strategic and technocratic leader (Marable 2007). As a lawyer, his style of communication was more formal and structured than the others mentioned here. Unlike these two other leaders, Patterson was a black Jamaican. Despite this, he managed to lead the PNP to more victories than any other leader in the modern Jamaican political context.

Edward Seaga emerged from the JLP as another technocratic leader who was a significant force in the Jamaican political landscape. His leadership style was autocratic (Stone 1992); however, his witty approach to political communication helped him to achieve several important political victories from 1980 to 1989.

Key Terms

For clarity and consistency, these terms will be used in the following ways in this book:

Americanization – The process of inculcating values and attitudes from the United States to individuals and societies that are not originally from there. This has been facilitated by globalization through the use of modern technologies. Important to this process is the media, which has acted as a pre-eminent conduit for transmitting American values and attitudes worldwide.

Capitalism – An economic system based on the private ownership of the means of production and their operation for profit. In this economic system, the private sector is required to play a dominant role and determines what is to be produced, how much is to be produced, when to produce and the price to charge for the goods or services produced.

Communism – A philosophical, social, political and economic ideology and movement whose ultimate goal is the establishment of a communist society, which is a socioeconomic order structured upon the common ownership of the means of production and the absence of social classes, money and the state.

Democratic socialism – A political and economic theory under which the means of production, distribution and exchange are owned or controlled by the people, and the opportunities of society are equally available to all. Under this system, there is a great emphasis on social policy to drive the development of people. In the context of this book, it is the model that was pursued by the Manley regime in the 1970s and the declared ideology of the PNP.

Economic liberalization – The lessening of government regulations and restrictions in an economy in exchange for greater participation by private entities. Jamaica embarked on a process of economic liberalization from the latter half of the 1980s until the early 2000s. This was a part of the strategy to modernize the economy and make it more competitive.

Effective communication – Although regarded as subjective, this occurs when the designed message reaches the intended audience and the interpretation of the message is close to or similar to that which was intended by the sender. Hall et al. (1973) articulated a process that they believed led to effective communication. They developed the encoder/decoder model, in which the communication process entailed production, circulation, consumption and reproduction. *Production* is the phase that deals with the design of the message. *Circulation* addresses the channels through which the messages are distributed. *Consumption* is the use of the message by the receiver, and *reproduction* deals with the means of feedback that is provided by the receiver of the message. Once the receiver interprets the message in the way it was intended by the sender, the process is deemed to be effective. Distortions indicate there are problems with the communication.

Globalization – The intensification of worldwide social relations linking distant places in such a way that local happenings are shaped by events occurring many thousands of miles away, and vice versa.

Jamaica – An island state located in the Caribbean Sea, approximately ninety miles south of Cuba and southeast of the Gulf of Mexico. It has a population of approximately 2.7 million inhabitants of diverse ethnic origins. Patois, the local dialect, is spoken by approximately 95 per cent of the population as a substitute for the officially recognized, dominant language of English.

Ever since the country gained independence in 1962, parliamentary democracy has been the form of government practised with regularly held elections to elect its governments. The two major political parties are the JLP and the PNP. Unlike the United Kingdom, Jamaica has a codified constitution in which basic civil liberties are enshrined. In this regard, it is important to note that the right to dissent and freedom of expression are deeply entrenched in its political culture. Fundamentally, this is significant here, as these are quintessential to the practice of political communication.

Lessons – What has been learned from a particular engagement or activity. In this context, the focus is on the programmes and policies introduced by leaders in Jamaica during the period 1972–2006, viewed from a political communications perspective.

Liberal democracy – The type of democracy practised in Jamaica, a political ideology and form of government in which representative democracy operates under the principles of liberalism. It is characterized by elections among multiple distinct political parties, separation of powers into branches of government, the rule of law, a market economy and equal protection of human rights and civil liberties.

Liberalization – The process by which states, to one degree or another, must lower and ultimately remove national barriers to the movement of capital and barriers to competition across states and within states, with regards to the movement of goods and services. The process of liberalization was primarily driven by external institutions such as the International Monetary Fund (IMF), World Bank and the World Trade Organization (WTO).

Market-driven economy – An economy where the prices of goods and services are determined by the market. In the context of Jamaica, this was part of the process of economic liberalization during the 1990s.

Mediated political communication – The flow of political information among political actors and citizens through diverse media channels.

Modern Jamaica – The period from 1972 to 2006, the era after Jamaica gained political independence and embarked on the liberalization of its economy, during which radical transformation took place in the media landscape. During this period, each of the three leaders discussed in this book was elected for two full terms.

Patron clientelistic – The nature of dependent relationships that develop between political leaders and their supporters. This reference was coined by Stone as he described the nature of the relationship between political leaders and supporters in Jamaica.

Political communication – "Any written or electronic statement, pamphlet, advertisement or other printed or broadcast matter or statement, communication or advertisement delivered or accessed by electronic means, including but not limited to the Internet, containing an explicit appeal for the election or defeat of a candidate." Such a communication is circulated to an audience substantially comprised of "persons eligible to vote for the candidate on whose behalf the appeal is directed" (Nagy 2001, 3). This is a relatively modern term in the realm of political science, and it refers to individuals' relations with one another on a political level. The definition restricts political communication to that of election campaigning and takes into consideration pre-election or postelection activity.

Hahn (2003) defined political communication as an ongoing argument in a society about politics. He believed that this dialogue revolved around freedom and order and was therefore a specific mode of communication relating to political conversations. It is generally utilized as a mass mobilization strategy by political leaders and their political organizations to communicate with citizens.

Political leadership – The art and science of making decisions on behalf of a country by politicians. Pope Francis, speaking to the US Congress in 2015, opined that "a good political leader is one who, with the interest of all in mind, seizes the moment in a spirit of openness and pragmatism.

A good political leader always opts to initiate processes rather than possessing spaces" (McGregor 2015). Political leaders must therefore exercise political leadership that will create processes which will result in the transformation of their societies.

Political socialization – The process by which members of society develop attitudes and feelings towards politics. In other words, political socialization amounts to political upbringing.

Privatization – The process of divesting government-owned assets to private individuals or companies.

Success or failure – The ability or inability of a political leader and his or her administration to communicate with and motivate or demotivate its citizens or supporters to participate in the political process. Here, the litmus test is the ability to win elections.

* * *

In chapter 1, the conceptual framework of political communication is presented, including the theoretical and philosophical issues that affect it; the nature of political culture and political communication in Jamaica, as well as the structure of its governmental communication; the analysis of the variables of economic development, the social order and the international and regional agenda; and political advertisement and campaigning. This chapter also examines the current situation as it relates to new media on the island and the impact of it on the democratic process.

The nature of the political culture as it relates to the various institutions which constitute political influence in Jamaica is highlighted in chapter 2, and the role of the family is explored. Attention is drawn to the trade unions and their nexus with the political parties, and emphasis is placed on the role of the media.

Chapter 3 looks at the structure of political communication in Jamaica, while chapter 4 explores the nature of the relationship between the leader and citizens, as well as the effect of economic programmes and policies on mass population.

Chapter 5 considers the introduction of social programmes to society, and then chapter 6 appraises Jamaica's regional and international outreach. There, some attention is paid to the method of communicating the country's stance regarding global issues and the population's reaction to this.

Chapter 7 explores the diverse approaches to political campaigning in depth and considers its evolution since independence. New media, political communication and citizen participation in the process are the focus of chapter 8, including the national response triggered by the introduction of the Internet.

Finally, chapter 9 presents a synopsis of the entire book, including the analysis of findings along with their recommendations and suggestions of opportunities for further research.

Disclosure

I am a known political affiliate of the PNP and have been an active participant in the political process of Jamaica since 1998. I was appointed a senator in the Parliament and then promoted to minister of state in the Ministry of Labour and Social Security in 2001. I served in those capacities until 2007, when there was a change of political administration. I was reappointed to the Parliament in 2012 as a senator, and in 2013 was promoted to president of the Senate. These parliamentary and government positions enabled acquisition of first-hand experience with implemented programmes and policies.

Given this context, conducting work on political communication while being an active participant in the political process was occasionally challenging, with some JLP interviewees cautious about responding because they were concerned that the information could be used against them in a political campaign.

However, every effort was made to adhere to the ethical standards required in qualitative work. As a result of my intimate knowledge of the workings of Parliament and government, I was able to triangulate qualitative data with documentary and other sources to avoid bias in the book. This allowed the data to drive the process and mitigated or prevented the inadvertent imposition of personal opinions on the findings, thus enhancing credibility.

Challenges were also presented in preparation of this text by the fact of my visual impairment. Happily, with my vast experience and the assistance of relevant technology, all obstacles were overcome, ending in the successful production of this book.

1.

The Conceptual Framework of Political Communication

Communication is extremely important in any political process, and in a modern context, no political parties or their leaders can be effective in communicating their programmes and policies without using the media. It is that institution that gives efficacy to what is being communicated, where the receiver interprets and understands messages in the same or a similar manner as the sender intends (Hall et al. 1973). If there are misunderstandings or misinterpretations by individuals, that suggests something is wrong with the process. Misunderstandings and misinterpretations of messages contribute to the failure of these leaders and institutions. Conversely, correct interpretations and understandings redound to their success.

Because this book explores the argument that "the success or failure of a leader and his or her political organization in Jamaica is closely linked to an effective communication strategy for their programmes and policies to citizens", there is a concentrated focus on the media and the process of communication.

Those who are charged with the responsibility of producing and disseminating the messages of political leaders and their political organizations must be cognizant of the process and what it entails.

They must ask the following questions:

- What is the relationship between leaders and the wider society they seek to influence?
- What are the communication methods and techniques that have been deployed in the exercise of power in relation to the perceived popular source of that power – the people?
- How is change effected or stymied by political communication?

They must also be conscious of some of the foundational ontological and epistemological issues driving political communication, such as freedom and order.

The concepts are quintessential, as they serve to highlight some of the central issues related to the subject. These ontological and epistemological issues are central to understanding and explaining some of the concerns involved in communicating messages from political leaders and their political organizations in Jamaica.

The dichotomy between *freedom* and *order* has been debated by scholars and philosophers from the time of Socrates, and more recently, other philosophers such as Thomas Hobbes, John Locke, Hahn and John Stuart Mill have differed in their points of view.

Hobbes believed that in the state of nature, men are "solitary, poor, nasty brutish and short". Because of this state of nature, he believed that the state had the right to preserve order and to restrict freedom (Hobbes [1651] 1969). Locke, on the other hand, believed that no one had the right to impose restrictions on another unless that person agreed to surrender his or her rights. If there were impositions, then people had the right to defend themselves. He maintained the view that the state should be there only to preserve the rights of citizens (Locke [1689] 1988).

In *On Liberty*, Mill offered some interesting perspectives. He discussed the historical struggle between authority and liberty and described the "tyranny" of government, which in his view needed to be controlled by the liberty of citizens (Mill [1859] 2010). He divided this control of authority into two distinct areas – necessary rights belonging to citizens and the "establishment of constitutional checks by which the consent of the community, or a body of some sort, supposed to represent its interest, was made a necessary condition to some of the more important acts of the governing power" (4). Mill cautioned against tyrannical rule, either from government or from the majority. He felt there were three fundamental liberties that must be preserved for individuals: freedom of thought and emotion; freedom to pursue taste, providing this did no harm to others, even if deemed immoral; and freedom to unite, so long as the involved members were of age and were not forced, and no harm was done to others (Mill [1859] 2010, 19).

Hahn (2003) articulated the concepts of freedom and order in the context of political communication and liberal democracy. He argued that political communication was related to a societal conversation taking place linked with politics. In this dialogue, the conversations revolved around freedom and order.

In the case of Jamaica, political conversations have been shaped by the political parties and the media, and in the case of the political parties, the issues of freedom and order are quite glaring.

Since 1938, two political parties have dominated Jamaican politics. Both have been influenced by their British counterparts: the PNP was aligned with the British Labour Party, a liberal political organization, and the JLP was aligned with the British Conservative Party, a conservative political organization. Accordingly, the principles and practices of the local political class and their political organizations have been adopted from their British counterparts and are best manifested in the programmes and policies implemented for the people.

What, therefore, is the reality of Jamaica's political system and culture? How do they help shape the communication strategies of leaders and their administrations? To what extent have the political system and culture helped to shape or stymie the practice of political communication in Jamaica? In answering these questions, arguments by Hobbes, Locke, Mill and Hahn explain some of the issues related to the practice of political communication in this country.

Effective Communication

But before examining those arguments, to determine the effectiveness of the communication strategies of the leaders and their political organizations, there must also be a lucid understanding of the political culture of the society under study. In this context, the work of Carl Stone obtains.

Stone, one of the foremost political scholars from Jamaica and the Caribbean, posited that Jamaica's political culture is deeply embedded with dependence on political leaders. He argued that a clientelistic relationship has developed, with three distinct players: the patron, the broker and the clients. The *patron* is the leader, who sits at the top and is seen as the ultimate provider for the broker and the client. The *broker* is the intermediary, who negotiates for benefits with the patron for the clients. Finally, the *clients* are citizens who depend on their leaders for scarce benefits (Stone 1980).

In designing any communication strategy, leaders must be cognizant of the political culture in the society. This culture, embracing attitudes, norms, practices and beliefs, is fundamental to developing programmes and policies that are responsive to the people and available for them to show appreciation to their leaders and administrations, who will determine success based on that appreciation.

Crucial to the actions of political leaders in creating and communicating programmes and policies to citizens is an understanding of human actions and behaviours involved in the concept of agency. According to Giddens (1984), *agency* refers to the capacity of individuals to act independently and make their own free choices based on their will. Human beings by nature are individualistic and have the capacity to act independently. This capacity to act independently and exercise free will is grossly manifested in liberal democracies that promote basic civil liberties. Jamaica is a liberal democratic state, and citizens strongly embrace their civil liberties. They sometimes express this freedom by abstaining from elections (over 40 per cent), thus causing concerns about the communication strategies being used by political leaders and their political organizations.

The behaviour of the Jamaican voting population is difficult to predict, and politicians must be conscious of this fact. There must be greater understanding of the audience (citizens) and the way they receive and consume messages. The communication strategies of leaders and their administrations must be sensitive to the needs of citizens, as it is this sensitivity that will engender greater responsiveness, and ultimately successful leadership and administration.

In this regard, media messaging and audience reception theories are significant. The works of Hall et al. (1973), Lasswell (1948) and McLuhan (1964), therefore, are instrumental to the understanding of the context.

Communication Models

Hall et al. (1973, 128) debated the communication models which prevailed at the time – linearity versus the cyclical: "Traditionally, mass communications research has conceptualized the process of communication in terms of a circulation circuit or loop. This model has been criticized for its linearity (sender/message/receiver), for its concentration on the level of message exchange and for the absence of a structured concept of the different moments as a complex structure of relations."

They suggested instead that the communication process entailed production, circulation, consumption and reproduction, which they crystallized as the encoder/decoder model of communication.

But they also saw that it was possible (and useful) to think of this process in terms of a structure produced and sustained through the articulation of linked but distinctive moments – production, circulation, distribution/consumption and reproduction. This means to think of the process as a "complex structure in dominance", sustained through the articulation of connected practices, Each of these, however, retained its distinctiveness and had its own specific modality – its own forms and conditions of existence (Hall et al. 1973, 128).

In this theoretical development, Hall and his colleagues submitted that the *production phase* deals with the design of the message; *circulation* entails the media through which the message is distributed; *consumption* refers to how the message is received and used by the receiver; and *reproduction* deals with the meaning ascribed to the message by the receiver and how it is repackaged and sent back to the sender. Accordingly, this constituted how the communication process contributes to effective communication. They further suggested that "it is in the discursive form that the circulation of the product takes place, as well as its distribution to different audiences. Once accomplished, the discourse must then be translated – transformed, again – into social practice as if the circuit is to be both completed and effective. If no 'meaning' is taken, there can be no 'consumption'. If the meaning is not articulated in practice, it has no effect" (Hall et al. 1973, 129).

Lasswell's (1948) model of communication defines an act of communication in terms of what was said, in what channel it was said, to whom it was said and with what effect it was said. But McLuhan (1964) noted that the medium, not the content, is really the message. He went on further to explain that a medium affects the society because it plays a role, not only by the content transmitted through the medium, but also by the characteristics of the medium itself. He also believed that it is the medium that shapes and controls the scale and form of human association and action.

His perspective of the medium in a very broad sense saw the light bulb as a clear example of his famous phrase, "The medium is the message." A light bulb does not have content the way a newspaper has articles or television has programmes, and yet it is a medium with social effects; that is, a light bulb enables people to create spaces during nighttime that would otherwise be enveloped by darkness. It was McLuhan's view that the "medium" is what gives effect to the message, as that is what determines how the message is transmitted, when it is transmitted, why it is being transmitted and who is transmitting it.

The theories of Hall et al., Lasswell and McLuhan are of fundamental importance. The media is one of the major institutions of socialization in Jamaican society, so it is a critical agent in the political communication process.

The ongoing dialogue on politics, as postulated by Hahn, takes place and is manifested in what political scholars consider the public sphere. Jürgen Habermas, one of the foremost scholars in the field of political communication, made seminal contributions through theories postulated in *Theory of Communicative Action* (1984) and *The Structural Transformation of the Public Sphere* (1989). From a socioscientific viewpoint, he posited that language is a medium for coordinating action, although it is not the only medium. The fundamental form of coordination through language requires speakers to adopt a practical stance oriented towards "reaching understanding", which he regarded as the "inherent telos" of speech. When actors address one another with this sort of practical attitude, they engage in "communicative action", which is distinguished from strategic forms of social action (Habermas 1984).

In communicative action, called "strong communicative action" in *Some Further Clarifications of the Concept of Communicative Rationality* (Habermas 1998), speakers coordinate their action and pursuit of individual (or joint) goals on the basis of a shared understanding that the goals are inherently reasonable or meritworthy. Where strategic action succeeds insofar as the actors achieve their individual goals, communicative action succeeds insofar as the actors freely agree that their goals are reasonable and merit cooperative behaviour. Communicative action is thus an inherently consensual form of social coordination in which actors "mobilize the potential for rationality", given the ordinary language and its telos of rationally motivated agreement.

Conversely, in strategic action, actors are not so much interested in mutual understanding as in achieving the individual goals they bring to the situation. Actor A, for example, will thus appeal to B's desires and fears so as to motivate behaviour on B's part that is required for A's success. As reasons motivating B's cooperation, B's desires and fears are only contingently related to A's goals. B cooperates with A, in other words, not because B finds A's project inherently interesting or worthy, but because of what B gets out of the bargain: avoiding some threat that A can make or obtaining something that A has promised (which may be of inherent interest to B, but for A is only a means of motivating B).

In determining the approaches that selected leaders of the Jamaican political process have utilized since 1972, both communicative action and strategic action are unequivocally important. Has the approach been consensual or strategic? In order to determine how successful the leaders and their political administrations will be, the communication means utilized must be anchored in either a consensual or a strategic mode.

Habermas's theory of the public sphere has also set the stage for a greater understanding of the issues involved in political communication, and it has been thoroughly examined and critiqued by international scholars. Indeed, the theory is a foundational anchor of this book.

His central argument is that discussion and dialogue about societal issues take place within the public sphere, and these discussions trigger and influence political actions. He described the public sphere as spaces where people can congregate, freely discuss and identify societal problems, and influence political action. These spaces include areas such as barbershops, coffeehouses, clubs and societies, and the media – newspaper, radio and television (Habermas 1989).

How relevant and applicable is this concept in the decision-making process of Jamaica? Do politicians pay attention to the views of citizens as expressed in the public sphere?

The thinking of Hahn, Habermas, Stone, Hall et al. and Giddens about freedom and order, the public sphere, communicative action, dependency and encoding, and decoding and agency set a foundation for understanding how political dialogue takes place within the context of liberal democracy in Jamaica. One can, therefore, integrate the concepts of freedom and order into notions of the public sphere, dependency and encoding, and decoding and agency to develop or explain the political communication typology for Jamaica.

In liberal democracies, discussions which take place within the private sphere revolve around freedom and order, resulting in the evolution of liberals and conservatives. Individuals often emerge from this private sphere with particular values and attitudes whose characteristics shape their perspectives on a range of subjects. It is this process of socialization that is manifested in the dialectics of the public sphere, resulting in people having the right to form their own opinions.

Discussions which occur in the public sphere are generally about issues such as economic development, the state of the social order, foreign policy, national security, property rights, political activism and the constitution. In *Polyarchy, Participation and Opposition,* Dahl (1971) described necessary prerequisites for democracy to thrive and for citizens to participate in the political process. These prerequisites appear in the dialogue in the public sphere and help to form the programmes and policies implemented by leaders and their political organizations.

In communicating these programmes and policies, political leaders have to develop a communication approach. This can be strategic (deliberate) communicative action, or it could be consensual. The programmes and policies then have to be packaged and transmitted to citizens in an efficient manner. The media is one institution that facilitates large-scale dialogue among leaders and citizens and amplifies the messages expressed by leaders and their political organizations to the broader population. But in designing these communication approaches, leaders and their political organizations must be conscious of the capacity of individuals to act independently and to make free choices. The programmes and policies, therefore, must cater to citizens' needs, as this is likely to solicit greater responsiveness.

To recap, the political communication dialectics (figure 1) in the context of Jamaica take into account the following theories and concepts:

1. *The preproduction phase,* where ideas, thoughts and opinions are formulated by citizens in their public spaces and are relayed to leaders and their political organizations.
2. *The production phase,* where the leaders and their political parties formulate programmes and policies based on information received from citizens. These are then packaged and communicated to citizens, as if the content originated from these leaders and their political organizations.
3. *The circulation phase,* where the message is disseminated to citizens via formal or informal media.

4. *The consumption phase,* where citizens receive the message and formulate their opinions. Citizens can accept or reject the message or be ambivalent towards it. In political terms, these are interpreted either through the lens of "liberal" or "conservative", or by those who have become sceptical about the political process.

5. *The reproductive phase,* where the messages are ascribed meaning and repackaged by citizens and re-sent to the leaders and their political organizations, directly or indirectly.

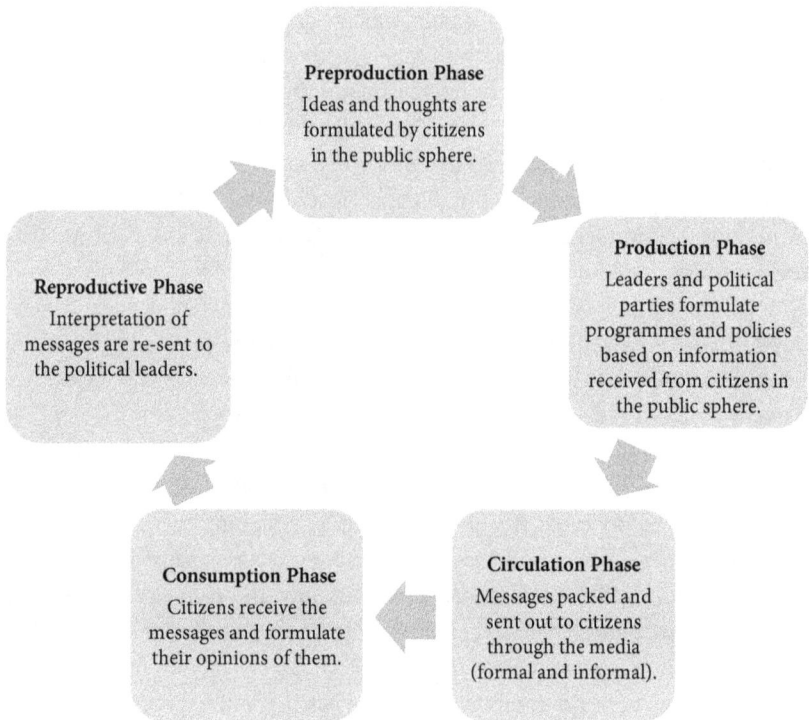

Figure 1. Conceptual map of political communication.
Source: Morris (2001).

2.

Political Culture and Political Communication in Jamaica

Blumler and Kavanagh (1999) describe three phases of political communication in a democracy. In the first phase, communication is centripetal, with citizens relying heavily on political parties and their leaders for information. In the second phase, there is less emphasis on transparency in government, and politicians still retain pride of place in their society. In the third phase, communication becomes more centrifugal, as there are more competing sources from which information can be secured in the public sphere. It is characterized by a proliferation in media and increased professionalization of individuals who design and interpret political messages.

Over the past fifty years, Jamaica has been experiencing an evolution in its political culture. In the early stages, the family, church, trade unions and political parties were the major institutions from which values, norms and social practices developed. This period coincided with what Blumler and Kavanagh (1999) depict as the early (or first) phase of political communication. The family, for example, was the institution to which the younger generation would look for influence and determine which political organization they should support. It is at the level of the family that the political dialogue on freedom and order is introduced and individuals choose a particular political ideology – liberal or conservative (Hahn 2003).

Simultaneously, political parties had a pride of place in the lives of Jamaicans, as they were a pre-eminent source of information dissemination and harvesting of scarce resources. The founders deliberately established mechanisms to transmit and receive information about programmes and policies that they were pursuing or wished to pursue in the country.

However, over the past twenty years, we have seen a change in the political culture of the society, and although the family and political parties are still regarded as major institutions of socialization, the media has emerged as a parallel institution of significance. It was ranked lower in the listing of institutions of socialization in the 1960s, but this situation has changed significantly since the 1990s, as the growth of modern technologies coupled with an aggressive economic liberalization and privatization programme contributed to an exponential growth of the media landscape (Brown 1998). This has resulted in Jamaicans shifting their loyalty and respect for certain authority figures and institutions. For example, it seems that more respect and loyalty are being shown to talk show hosts than to politicians (Rosenberg 1999), and levels of support for political parties and trade unions are changing (Powell, Bourne and Waller 2007). More individuals are now influenced by the media than these organizations (Rodriquez 1996). The means of communication have become more centrifugal (third phase) than centripetal (first phase).

These changes must also be seen within the context of a broader global perspective. Other exogenous factors, such as the collapse of communism (Munroe 2002) and the rapid move towards a globalized world, have forced societies to change the way they think and their attitudes towards development (Giddens 1991). Homogenization of media systems throughout the world has meant that they have been required to play a fundamental role in linking different cultures, thus leading to a shift in certain traditional values and attitudes. Therefore, in Jamaica, as elsewhere, the media must be seen as a fundamental institution in any assessment of political communication, as it serves to shape the values, norms, personalities and attitudes of individuals within the public sphere.

For any leader or political organization to design an effective communication programme, they have to understand the political culture of the society – the way that people think and how they are likely to react to initiatives that are presented – and that this is dynamic and subject to change from time to time. This is quintessential for the production phase of any message design, as articulated by Hall et al. (1973).

Political culture involves the teaching of values such as respect for authority, loyalty, love for country and respect for democratic principles, including the various civil liberties and the respect for law and order.

Similarly, for effective communication of government programmes and policies, a lucid understanding of the values, norms, attitudes and morals of the society, transmitted to individuals through institutions such as the family, church, educational institutions, trade unions, political parties, the media and peer groups, is critical. These intrinsic values and attitudes are born out of a process known as *political socialization* (Munroe 2002; Stone 1992), the comprehension of which, according to Stone (1992), is a necessity in the study of the politics of a society. Therefore, for a political administration to communicate effectively with its citizens, there must be a clear understanding of their values, norms, traditions, attitudes and practices, as these will determine political behaviour.

Stone (1980) described the political culture of Jamaica as being patron clientelistic, as it is a culture born out of dependency. A relationship emerges among leaders and citizens in which there is a patron at the top, a broker in the middle and a client at the bottom. The patron is the maximum leader/prime minister; the broker is the member of Parliament and the client is the citizen (Stone 1980). This relationship will be examined further to determine the impact that it has had on the practice of political communication in the country.

The values and attitudes of citizens manifest themselves in the dialogue that transpires in the public sphere – an area in public life where people can come together and freely discuss and identify societal problems, and by doing so, influence political action. Individuals tend to proffer political arguments in areas and spaces where they are comfortable and dependent on how they are socialized politically.

Previously, it has been pointed out that political communication developed as a result of the ongoing dialogue that was taking place around politics in the public sphere, related to freedom and order. The freedom argument is centred on the belief that all humans are born free and no government has the right to impose restrictions on the lives of these individuals. The argument for order reflects the belief that for civilization to take place, order must be imposed so that people can enjoy their freedom.

Both arguments have resulted in the classification of liberal democracy (Munroe 2002) into two distinct groups – liberals and conservatives (Hahn 2003) – which emerge from the different institutions of socialization and are supposed to assist in shaping the communication strategies of leaders and their administrations. It is from this debate that we seek to understand the Jamaican perspective.

In research for the Centre of Leadership at the University of the West Indies, Powell, Bourne and Waller (2007) found that approximately 53 per cent of those Jamaicans surveyed favoured freedom, as opposed to 43 per cent who opted for order. This seemed to indicate that Jamaicans preferred freedom to order. In that same study, approximately 76 per cent of Jamaicans supported democracy as the best system of government. While approximately 57 per cent of the respondents believed that it was only through democracy that Jamaica could become a developed country, 59 per cent stated that they would not support a military government "if things became bad". These results indicate that as a group, Jamaicans have great regard for democracy and democratic values are deeply entrenched within the society. Undoubtedly, this is because of the process of socialization, strongly linked to liberal democracy, which emerged from British colonialism.

The Family

It is an established fact that in virtually all societies, the family constitutes one of the major institutions of socialization. This is the first point of contact for people, where certain values and attitudes are transmitted and practised. According to Rodriquez (1996), approximately 97 per cent of Jamaicans held this to be true, outlining the family rules of engagement and determining what was right and wrong, as well as indicating that the family was regarded as an integral part of society. It is through this institution that people are first exposed to authority figures and norms, such as the view that each family ought to be headed by two parents. It is through institutions such as the family that certain political beliefs are born and transferred. In Jamaica, for example, where there is intense loyalty to the two major political parties, the PNP and the JLP, support is generally linked to family traditions, although there have been signs of changes in this behaviour in recent years. Evidently, this change is becoming more obvious as citizens engage in a battle for economic survival and there is an increase in educational opportunity to a greater cross section of the Jamaican population.

In the context of political communication, it is within the family that major political discourse is born. Family members who are exposed to political parties are generally vocal about political matters in the home, where certain values and beliefs about the political process are inculcated. It is here that the debate about freedom and order begins. It must also be noted that it is in the homes of family members that the grass-roots organizational structures of the political parties in Jamaica are formed. In interviews with the elite leaders of the political parties, they confirmed that their political views had been shaped by family orientation.

Trade Unions

Trade unions play an invaluable role in the cultivation of the political culture of virtually all Western democracies, where they hold pride of place in the political process. Workers' rights and conditions of work for the labourers within these societies are at the forefront of trade union advocacy and in most of these areas, they are aligned with specific political parties. For example, the Trades Union Congress in Britain, which is an umbrella organization for most of the significant trade unions, is aligned with the British Labour Party. A similar culture exists in Jamaica. The country's two major trade unions, the National Workers Union and the Bustamante Industrial Trade Union, are affiliate members of the PNP and JLP, respectively.

From these associations, workers developed loyalty to the trade unions and their leaders, and by extension, to the political parties with which the unions were associated; and members formed the base support of the parties in the emergent stages of Jamaica's political development. In most instances, trade union members have delegate status in the associated political parties, and their special privilege can influence the policy directions of the political parties, and by extension, the government. Political leaders of the country have been privy to this practice and acknowledge that it has played a role in formulating their communication strategies.

Trade unions also affect the political culture of society through the influence of leadership in the political process. Leaders evolved from trade unions, which has regularly affected the implementation of government programmes and policies. In Jamaica, union leaders such as Norman Manley and Michael Manley of the National Workers Union and Alexander Bustamante and Hugh Shearer of the Bustamante Industrial Trade Union became leaders of the government during the first twenty years of Jamaica gaining political independence.

The transition of trade union leaders into leaders of government has contributed to the creation of strong labour laws to protect workers' rights and dignity. The Employment Termination and Redundancy Act of 1974 and the Labour Relations and Industrial Disputes Act are two examples. Hence, trade unions provide an important platform for the communication of programmes and policies to workers.

Since the 1990s, Jamaica has witnessed a transition in the influence of trade unions. This can be attributed to two considerable factors: the change in configuration of the economy and change in leadership personalities. Prior to 1990, the Jamaican economy was largely closed, as it was heavily dependent on products such as sugarcane, banana and bauxite. In these sectors, there was heavy dependence on manual labour, so there was a muscular presence within trade unions. However, since the diversification of the economy, with an increasing trend towards the service industries, there has been a noticeable reduction in their influence. Two of the subjects of this book's focus, Edward Seaga and P.J. Patterson, did not have leadership roles in the trade union movement. Their leadership of the country came at a time when the economy was diversified.

The absence of strong and dynamic leadership personalities undoubtedly contributed to the diminishing influence of the trade unions. Workers had developed a passionate following of trade union leaders such as Norman Manley, Michael Manley, Bustamante and Shearer because of their charisma. This helped to consolidate their positions in their respective political parties.

Powell et al. (2007) indicated that some trade union leaders who eventually became prime ministers had enjoyed high approval ratings before their election. Of the six national leaders with approval ratings of between 80 and 90 per cent, three – Norman Manley, Michael Manley and Bustamante – were heads of trade unions and later became prime ministers. However, since their departure from the political landscape, no other trade union leader has ascended to that office.

Political Parties

Political parties are vital actors in the liberal democratic process. They are organizations which engage in contests for political power to get the right to govern a society. The principle and practice of political competition are thus deeply embedded in a successful democracy. This principle and practice have also been deeply entrenched in the political culture of Jamaica.

Political parties strengthen the dialogue on freedom and order, which intensifies as they seek to distinguish themselves from each other. This distinction is accomplished by adopting certain core principles. In the PNP, these principles revolved around democratic socialism (PNP 1978), in contrast to the JLP's focus on capitalism (Stone 1989b).

Over the years, political parties have embarked on a deliberate strategy to market these core ideas to their supporters. Scholars such as Lippmann (1922) and Bernays (1928) regarded these ideals as propaganda, defined as "a consistent, enduring effort to create or shape events to influence the relations of a public to an enterprise, idea, or group" (Lippmann 1922, 25). Both the PNP and the JLP utilize "groups" and branches as the basic mechanism for communicating with citizens. These are the major conduits for transmitting their propaganda, and the messages are communicated in the context of their political ideology. Both the PNP and the JLP have been enmeshed in the political dialogue on "freedom" and "order", with the PNP adopting a more liberal perspective and the JLP a more conservative one (Panton 1993).

Groups and branches are extremely important organs of the political parties in Jamaica, and in some instances they are entrenched in their respective constitutions (JLP 2003; PNP 2008). In the context of political communication, they act as an extensive source of information dissemination (the circulation phase) as well as the point of providing feedback (the reproduction phase). These are significant phases in the communication process as adumbrated by Hall et al. (1973).

The PNP and the JLP have established constitutional mechanisms to guide the operations of their organizations, as discussed next.

The People's National Party

In the context of the PNP, the constitution outlines their modus operandi. Groups make up the base of the organization and are formed within polling divisions. All groups fall within parish council divisions, which make up the constituency and are governed by an executive committee. This is headed by a chairman who is normally the member of Parliament (PNP 2008). All constituencies fall within a region. There are six regions within the PNP, and each has a regional executive committee, which is headed by a chairman.

The National Executive Council (NEC) is the highest decision-making body outside of the PNP's annual conference. The day-to-day operations are governed by the executive committee, which comprises the president, four vice presidents, chairman, general secretary, two deputy general secretaries, six regional chairmen, eleven elected representatives from the NEC, two representatives from the PNP Youth Organisation, two representatives from the PNP Women's Movement, three representatives from the National Workers Union and four coopted members.

The NEC comprises members of the executive committee, elected representatives from the regional executive committees, members of Parliament, senators and selected representatives from arms and affiliates such as the PNP Youth Organisation, the National Workers Union and the PNP Women's Movement (PNP 2008).

Outside of the NEC, the annual conference is the highest decision-making body. At that meeting, any amendment to the constitution can be made and the president and four vice presidents are elected. The constitution gives the right to delegates to move and debate resolutions on any matter that is of national importance or of significance to the PNP as an organization (PNP 2008).

These structures, as outlined in the constitution, are extremely important in this discussion. It gives a vivid understanding of the kind of organization that allows citizens to participate in the political dialogue, which is critical to the study of any political communication, as there must be forums for dialogue in any democratic system.

The Jamaica Labour Party

The JLP also has a constitution, with structures in place for the operation of the organization. From its inception, the organization has focused heavily on the guidance and influence of its leader. This was the case under the leadership of Alexander Bustamante (from 1943 to 1974) and Edward Seaga (from 1974 to 2005).

At the base of the party are individuals joined together in branches. These branches select delegates to represent their views at different levels of the

JLP. Their constitution also provides for the establishment of divisional and constituency executives. However, since the 1970s, these have not functioned consistently. Bruce Golding, a former leader and general secretary of the party, pointed out that the organization made changes in the 1970s because the branch network, constituency and divisional executives were not functioning effectively. A system was installed to select delegates in accordance with the number of elected votes that the party received in a constituency during the last general election. The views expressed by Golding were supported by another former general secretary, Karl Samuda. According to him, when he assumed the role of general secretary in 2003, there were approximately 100 branches, but they were not functioning effectively.

The JLP has four major regions, which are known as *area councils*. These are led by a chairman, and each area council is assigned one of the four deputy leaders. The area councils are allowed to elect the deputy leaders of the JLP. The highest decision-making body outside of the annual conference is the Central Executive. This body comprises members of Parliament, senators, representatives from JLP's youth arm (known as Young Jamaicans) and selected members from other affiliated groups and members of the standing committee. The Standing Committee is the body that oversees the party's daily operation and ensures that the decisions of the Central Executive are implemented (JLP 2003).

On the political scale, the Central Executive would be the equivalent to the NEC of the PNP. The Central Executive, like the NEC, cannot amend the constitution without taking it to its annual conference. It can propose amendments, but they must be approved by delegates at the All-Island General Council or annual conference. The All-Island Annual General Council is where the party leader is elected if necessary. It is an avenue for the leadership of the organization to report to its supporters on issues related to the party and to the country as a whole.

Dialogue and Decision-Making

One of the major reasons for the establishment of these structures within the two dominant political parties by their founders is to facilitate political dialogue among its members. Branches and groups are meant to be the engine of these political organizations; they keep them alive on the ground. They are the mechanisms that assist in marketing the programmes and policies of the political parties and accommodate the indoctrination of members in the communities where they are located. Furthermore, they are designed to provide feedback to the political parties on the effectiveness (or lack thereof) of the programmes and policies being implemented. They are a vital means of communication for the political parties. According to Section 31.6–7 of the PNP's constitution, two of the primary functions of the group are "Policy discussion and formulation" and "Participation in the Party's internal democratic processes and decision-making" (PNP 2008).

For these roles to be fulfilled, the groups must have access to information from their leaders, and the leaders in turn must be prepared to allow them to participate in the policymaking process. The leadership of the groups and branches within the communities, in the embryonic stage, were professionals who had at least a decent education and were able to read and write. They were the ones who would receive and distil complex policy decisions in a simple format to citizens in their communities. Group leaders and branches transmitted information to residents and received feedback via person-to-person communication. This coincided with Blumler and Kavanagh's (1999) observation of the first phase of political communication in a democracy. Communication was more centripetal, as citizens relied heavily on the political parties and their leaders for information.

However, there has been a significant decline in the operations of these branches and groups. Until 2005, there were fewer than one thousand registered groups within the PNP, with fewer than two thousand delegates. Concurrently, there was no available information on functioning branches in the JLP. This coincides with the third phase of political communication in democracy, during which communication becomes more centrifugal, as there are more competing sources from which information can be secured in the public sphere. Therefore, one can understand the problem that both political organizations have experienced with communicating the programmes and policies that their governments sought to implement. According to Maxine Henry-Wilson, a former general secretary of the PNP (personal communication), these organs of the political parties have been relegated to being mere election-mobilizing mechanisms; they have diverted significantly from their original intent, as established by their founding fathers in 1938 and 1943.

The virtual emasculation of the group and branch structures of the political parties in Jamaica has contributed to the growing disenchantment with them among citizens. The major political means of transmitting information in the communities and back to the political leaders have malfunctioned or been destroyed, and a vacuum has been created. In the interim, the political parties have not undertaken any reforms to their groups or branches, nor have they implemented replacement mechanisms or structures to fulfil the vital communication role that these organs play in national development.

Between obtaining the right to vote in 1944 and the end of the period under review (2006), Jamaica held fourteen national elections, with the PNP and JLP sharing the honour of governing the country on different occasions. The PNP governed for eight terms to the JLP's six. While competing for political power, they developed support bases, drawn from different sectors within the society. These sectors shared the beliefs and practices of the respective political organizations. Supporters over time developed strong loyalty to the parties and their leaders, and they would go to any extent to ensure that their party won an election. They did so with the belief that upon securing political power, their party in return would implement programmes and policies beneficial to them. In some cases, an exploitative relationship emerged, whereby scarce benefits were allotted to individuals by politicians with the goal of maintaining their political power base. This reflects Stone's (1980) patron-clientelism construct and is thought to be widely practised in Jamaica.

The greater the loyalty and respect shown to the broker by clients, the more opportunities are presented to them. Such practices have resulted in a society deeply divided along political lines, as politicians seek to provide scarce benefits to those citizens who are closest to the party in power, with the aim of securing a positive election outcome.

But a series of legislative reforms took place designed to transform the electoral system and eradicate tribal politics. Buddan (2007, G3), writing in the *Gleaner* on 12 August, described the resulting political trajectory in Jamaica: "From 2002, the administration of the electoral system has provided a truer expression of voting behaviour and this is expected to continue in 2007. Voters' lists are cleaner, there is less over-voting and laws are in place to punish open voting. Election workers are also of better quality. These corrections will also redefine how we understand voting behaviour, measured in terms of the final count."

His arguments, however, reflected only recent developments in the political landscape and came within the context of the posteconomic liberalization era. Economic liberalization (Munroe 2002) had undoubtedly contributed to a shift in Jamaica's political culture because it reduced the amount of resources available to political actors. But Buddan (2007, G3) went further: "Beginning in 2002, the size of a party's popular support, seat margins won and balance of seats won have seen corrections to the point that the overall balance of strength between the parties is as competitive as in the period from 1949 to 1972. This is reinforced by the fact that the parties are more similar as the kinds of pragmatic parties they were in the 20-year period then."

The argument of Stone (1980), however, is a representation of the pre-economic liberalization period (that is, the era leading up to 1990), the second phase of political communication in democracy, where there is less emphasis on transparency in government and politicians still retain pride of place in their society.

The patron-client relationship that emerged in Jamaica in the 1970s contributed to a poisoning of the political discourse in society. Deep political conflicts emerged as individuals struggled for social and economic survival. A significant portion of the population hinged their existence on the political party they supported. The patron-clientelist culture contributed to the formation of "garrison constituencies" and the proliferation of "dons". Justice James Kerr (1997, 7), in his report on political tribalism, pointed out that garrison constituencies have resulted in

- increased difficulty in maintaining law and order;
- an inability to maintain social infrastructure (roads, water, sewage, garbage disposal, electricity, shops, supermarkets, markets), which border or pass through disparate communities;
- a restriction of movement through these areas, which affects human rights, transportation, and job attendance and opportunities; and
- a restriction of business opportunities to the localized area as customers from other communities are denied access by blocked roads and real or perceived threats of violence.

By 1980, these practices had climaxed, and the country had become polarized. The conflict resulted in more than eight hundred Jamaicans being killed in the lead-up to the national elections of that year.

The practice of the patron-clientelist political culture in Jamaica was largely evident in the first phase of political communication in democracy. This period was dominated by political parties which controlled the flow of information to and from citizens. During this phase, the media was less pervasive, and politicians played a more prominent role in the governance process. According to Janda and Colman (1998), this period lasted globally for the first twenty years of the post–Second World War era. It, however, lasted much longer in Jamaica.

Since the early 1990s, the country has seen a shift in the practice of patron-clientelism. The collapse of communism, the rapid move towards globalization and the expansion of the media, coupled with a growing debt problem, have minimized the level of resources available to governments (Munroe 1999). Consequently, they are now compelled to manage public resources more efficiently, which means that there is less incentive to give to the party faithful. The result is a reduction in core support for the political parties in Jamaica, which best manifests itself in the challenges confronting the group and branch structures.

Coincidentally, this shift came about during the 1990s and marked the third phase of political communication in democracy. In this period, the media was liberalized in Jamaica and a plethora of media institutions emerged.

The tightening of resources available to politicians and the increased scrutiny being placed on political actors could explain one of the findings by Powell and colleagues (2007). Pertaining to the level of satisfaction about the workings of democracy in Jamaica, the authors found that a significant group (64 per cent) were not satisfied, while a mere 33 per cent were. Citizens have grown increasingly disappointed in the performance of their governments because their expectations are higher than the reality.

These views are further borne out by the level of support for a market-driven economy. Approximately 60 per cent of the respondents from the Powell et al. (2007) study did not favour a market economy. This presents a major political communication dilemma and offers further theoretical insights into Stone's theory of patron-clientelism. The patron-client political culture which emerged out of the politics practised since independence in 1962 has moved to the establishment of a market economy, marking a fundamental shift from a mixed economy and the established political culture. The market economy has contributed to the liberalization of the media, freeing the people from the information stranglehold once maintained by politicians and political parties. More citizens have become enlightened by the media, thus contributing to the dissatisfaction. Therefore, the finding that 64 per cent of respondents were dissatisfied with the workings of democracy points to a serious political communication deficit. This must be remedied by policymakers for satisfaction levels of citizens to improve.

Since the collapse of communism, we have also seen a shift in the ideological posturing of many global political organizations which have moved towards adopting market-driven economies, thus contributing to the development of capitalist societies (Giddens 1991). This has been the experience of Jamaica since the early 1990s.

In the context of political communication, the embryonic stages of modern political development in Jamaica established clear distinctions between the two leading political organizations. Ideology formed a fundamental part of public policy during the 1970s and 1980s, the pinnacle of the Cold War. The PNP's focus was "freedom", having adopted a democratic socialist posture from their liberal democratic parent organization in the United Kingdom, the Labour Party (Patterson 2018). Conversely, the JLP tended towards "order", as they adopted a capitalist outlook and aligned themselves with conservative political organizations such as the Conservative Party (Seaga 2009).

The PNP, through its democratic socialist rhetoric, has consistently identified with freedom in the political dialogue. This is manifested through its emphasis on providing social services such as health and education to Jamaicans at either minimal or no cost. Such ideological posturing formed a tenet of the Michael Manley regime of the 1970s (Panton 1993). Conversely, the JLP has been seen as the party which identified with order, through their emphasis on managing the economy under a capitalist system. Their emphasis was more on growing the economy and less on providing social services to citizens. This was the ideological stance of the Seaga regime of the 1980s (Stone 1989b). These two distinguishing features of the major political parties were vividly demonstrated in the slogans of the campaigns of 1989. The PNP used the theme "We put people first", and the JLP countered with "It takes cash to care."

In 1989, however, with the return of the PNP to power, Jamaicans saw a variation in their ideological posture. The socialist dogma of the 1970s, led by Manley, was minimized and a greater emphasis placed on market-oriented policies. This made it difficult for the electors to distinguish between the philosophies of the two dominant parties. Undoubtedly, this contributed to the growing numbers of uncommitted voters because they could not make any fundamental distinction between the PNP and JLP. Both political parties have had to resort to serious political marketing to mobilize their supporters. The country thus has seen greater efforts to use political communication techniques to attract supporters in the decades since the 1990s.

The growth of a flourishing drug trade also served to minimize politicians' control of their constituencies. Individuals who engaged in this accumulated significant wealth, and in a context where the politicians are faced with reduced access to state resources, these narco-traders have been replacing politicians or contributing to partnerships. Such dangerous trends have seen the growth of gangs headed by so-called dons and have resulted in battles for turf, contributing to the high crime rate in Jamaica. This worrying development, according to Munroe (1999), has profound implications for the survival of democracy and the nation-state. A continued reduction in the influence of political leaders in their communities will undoubtedly result in an increase in the influence of undesirables such as dons on young people. One newspaper article underscored this point: "Jamaica is not unique in the infiltration of drug money into politics to buy protection and influence for dealers. But unsavoury elements of our politics, particularly the links to gangs and dons and the garrisonisation of communities, substantially increase our vulnerability" ("Drug Money and Politics", Gleaner, 11 February 2003, A4).

Notwithstanding the challenges that confront political parties in Jamaica, they have managed to maintain a core support among the population. Currently, base support for political parties stands at an approximate average of 20 per cent. According to the survey conducted by Powell et al. (2007), 24.4 per cent of respondents indicated that they consistently voted for the PNP, while 8.9 per cent said that they always voted for the JLP. This confirms the view that the PNP has a larger hard-core base than the JLP. Responding to the question, "Thinking back to the times you've voted in the past . . . how did you vote?" some 24.4 per cent reported that they "always" voted for the PNP, 10.5 per cent said they "usually" voted for the PNP, 8.7 per cent said they "always" voted for the JLP, and 6.7 per cent said they "usually" voted for the JLP, with another 10.8 per cent indicating they had voted for "both". This still leaves 38.9 per cent in the "Don't Know/No Answer category" (Powell et al. 2007).

The hard-core group of the political parties is held together by the established group and branch structures within both of them, and it is also supported by annual conferences that are designed to act as a rallying mechanism for grass-roots adherents. These mechanisms form a major part of the political culture and provide a fertile opportunity for political leaders to develop their communication strategies and communicate with their supporters. A theoretical argument can thus be extrapolated from the Jamaican experience. Citizen participation and satisfaction in the democratic process will depend on the nature of the political culture and the extent to which leaders develop their communication strategies and communicate policy changes. It is being argued that if there is effective communication, participation and satisfaction will be high. Conversely, if communication is poor, participation and satisfaction will be low.

The Media

A detailed examination of the role of the media is imperative for an in-depth understanding of the subject of political communication because it is through this means that most decisions taken by governments are transmitted to citizens. It is also through the media that dialogue on freedom and order is manifested, and through which the political parties channel their propaganda (Lippmann 2004). The media, therefore, plays a quintessential role in the development of the democratic process, and hence has a heavy impact on the political culture.

In the public sphere, the major role of the media is to educate, inform and entertain. These are important functions of any socializing agent. The information disseminated assists in shaping the values, morals, attitudes and practices within a society. For the purposes of this volume, the media consists of newspapers, television, radio, cinema and the Internet.

According to Hallin and Mancini (1998), improvements in technology, coupled with the increasing aggressiveness of journalists and growing commercialization, have contributed to the media's emergence as a major social force. Its influence has probably superseded the role of other social institutions such as the church, trade unions, peer groups and political parties.

Over the years, the media has played a leading role in the socializing process and retained pride of place in Jamaican society. The country has consistently operated and practised liberal democracy, making it a fertile environment within which the media can operate. Basic civil liberties are enshrined in its constitution through the Charter of Fundamental Rights and Freedoms, providing citizens with the right to freedom of expression and the right to dissent (Houses of Parliament 2011). Freedom House, an international body, has consistently ranked Jamaica in the top twenty countries in Latin America with significant press freedom (Freedom House 2015). Accordingly, Jamaica can be classified as an open democratic society in which the media and citizens are allowed freedom of speech and thought.

Newspapers

Prior to the pervasive use of radio, the dominant source of information was the newspaper. The downside to this was the population's low literacy rate. As a result, people had to depend on a literate member of the community to read and transfer information to them. Accessing information was seen as a major social activity, and literate community members who were able to read were revered.

The *Daily Gleaner*, established in 1834, was one of the first media organizations in Jamaica. Over the years, the publication became a household name, and it is still in operation. Citizens retained a strong loyalty to the publication, which probably explains its longevity. It currently has a readership base of over four hundred thousand and is the most read newspaper in the island (PIOJ 2013). Since then, Jamaica has seen the establishment of several other newspapers, such as the *Daily News* and the *Jamaica Record*, both of which have since ceased operations. The only major competitor to the *Gleaner* currently is the *Jamaica Observer*.

Newspapers have played a pivotal role in the development of Jamaica's political culture. They assumed the responsibility as watchdogs for democracy and took this quite seriously, with publishers gambling and persisting in their fight to ensure that the right to freedom and liberty is preserved. During the 1970s, for example, when it was felt that the Manley regime was too close to Fidel Castro's regime in Cuba, the *Daily Gleaner* placed a lot of pressure on the government to sever ties with it. A sour relationship emerged between the administration and the paper, which resulted in organized protests against each other. Some scholars felt that the *Daily Gleaner* played an inestimable role in the demise of the Manley regime during the 1980 elections (Stephens and Stephens 1986). Jamaicans' fear of communism ran rampant through society and was highly publicized in the *Daily Gleaner.*

This agenda-setting (McCombs and Shaw 1972) meant a constant focus on the subject of Jamaica's relationship with communist regimes, with regular headlines in the *Daily Gleaner.* The publication's repeated treatment of this important issue contributed to increased political activity, which eventually led to the Manley regime being voted out of office (Stone 1981). It is posited that the consistent exposure to news and images of communism – regarded as "citizen priming", a psychological effect that emerges after constant exposure to particular stimuli in the media (Price and Tewksbury 1997) – strongly contributed to the citizens' actions.

Radio

The world advent of radio in 1895, followed by television in 1927, detracted from the prestige which had been accorded to the newspaper (the second phase of political communication in democracy). People now had other sources of information which, being in audio and visual formats, were less difficult to understand. However, in the embryonic stages, the prohibitive cost meant that only the privileged few possessed these technologies, and so people gathered at strategic points in their communities to watch and listen to the news via these forms of media. This became another social event, with the only difference being the mode of transmission.

The development of transistors, and then transmitters, represented a major revolution in how individuals communicated with each other. It gave ordinary citizens an opportunity to access information in diverse formats which were unfathomable, and it ushered in a new era for communication globally.

Radio became a part of Jamaican society in the late 1940s and the first radio station was known as ZQI (the first phase of political communication in Jamaican democracy). It was later transformed into Radio Jamaica and Rediffusion (RJR) and became one of the leading radio stations. Another radio station, the Jamaica Broadcasting Corporation (JBC), was formed in 1959. It was owned by the government and later offered television services as well as radio. Over the years, both RJR and JBC played pivotal roles in shaping the political culture of the society, as they introduced programmes that served to empower Jamaican citizens. Both radio stations introduced talk shows where citizens could call in and articulate their views on any public matter or solicit help for problems they were experiencing in their communities. This allowed the two stations to influence the policies and programmes being formulated by their government. The hosts of these radio programmes have developed networks to respond to the needs of citizens, and most Jamaicans hold them in high regard. According to Matthew Rosenberg (1999), "These days, the free-wheeling medium increasingly is an outlet for frustrations with politicians' misdeeds and the government's inability to stem violence and crime or ease poverty." Rosenberg further articulated the views of once popular talk show host, Barbara Gloudon, as follows: "In the field, on the bus, in the office, in cars, in factories, in market places, people listen to the radio all day" (Rosenberg 1999).

Television

While radio was growing as a communications medium, television was introduced in 1963 through Jamaica Broadcasting Corporation Television (JBC TV). This provided another means of disseminating information to citizens and also played an indelible role in Jamaica's march towards political independence (Dunn 2005).

The novelty of television provided a means by which citizens could associate faces with the voices of their political leaders, which served to intensify their loyalty. A number of party functionaries in the rural constituencies, for example, could be seen and heard imitating both Norman Manley and Alexander Bustamante at street meetings.

In the early stages of Jamaica's development, the media could be construed as an ordinary institution of socialization. Indeed, the political parties were recognized more as a major socializing agent by citizens prior to 1980. One reason for this was the fact that a significant number of Jamaicans had no access to radio and television sets, were illiterate, or both (Stone 1992).

Economic liberalization and privatization (Munroe 2002) in the late 1980s resulted in an exponential growth of the media landscape and set the stage for the emergence of the third phase of political communication in democracy. Brown highlighted this development as he argued that the rapid progress towards regionalization made the Caribbean Basin Initiative, a US tariff programme, an attractive proposition to Caribbean countries like Jamaica. This initiative by the then Ronald Reagan administration was intended to facilitate trade among countries within the Caribbean and to stimulate much-needed economic growth. However, Brown further noted that in order for Caribbean countries to access the Caribbean Basin Initiative, they had to introduce a number of structural adjustments to their economies through privatization and divestment of multiple state-run entities. This precipitated the liberalization of the media industry in Jamaica (Brown 1998).

The two major national newspapers still existed, but there was also significant growth in community newspapers. Radio expanded from the two major traditional stations, with twenty-five additional stations launching by 2015. Television saw the addition of two national stations as well, increasing that number to three. Also, there were more than forty licensed operators on the island providing cable services to residents (Dunn 2005).

The Internet

However, the most significant addition to the media landscape in Jamaica was the Internet. This served to revolutionize the way that citizens communicated and conducted business with each other. For example, more and more people were using the Internet to transmit messages to each other. According to Dunn (2011), approximately 40 per cent of the population had access to the Internet at that time, and this figure is scheduled to grow exponentially as the telecommunication sector is further liberalized.

The introduction of the Internet contributed to the transformation of the media industry and levelled the playing field as it related to knowledge. Everyone, once they had access to the technology, could obtain information on virtually any subject on their own. Prior to this, they had to depend on some authority figure to access, translate and then disseminate information to them. To a large extent, this old method of accessing information limited citizens' ability to maximize their true potential.

Brown (1998, 50) remarked on the effect of the technological phenomenon:

> Another simultaneous technological development that was to have irreversible impact globally was the emergence of the personal computer (PC) as a consumer technology in the early 1980s. The subsequent convergence of telecommunications, computer and television technologies, has transformed in less than a generation, human society. The essential feature of the new age is that information is now a generic commodity – digitized bits of machine-readable data that can be bought and sold like any other commodity.

The Internet has thus served to educate, inform and entertain anyone who has access to it, and the greater the access to information, the more informed decisions a citizen is likely to make. Information gathering is projected to increase with the phenomenal growth in cellular phones and land-based telephone lines, both of which are handy for accessing the Internet. According to the Planning Institute of Jamaica (2013), approximately 80 per cent of the Jamaican population (more than two million people) have access to either form of phone. The growth of the Internet has also facilitated the increase of chat rooms – virtual spaces where people can communicate privately – which are particularly popular among young people, who use them to connect with their peers.

The liberalization of the media industry in Jamaica has contributed considerably to the transformation of the political culture. Prior to 1980, the political parties through their groups or branches were a major source of information. However, the media has put significant competitive pressure on these bodies, ultimately contributing to a decline in core support for them. Prior to 1980, for example, core support for the political parties hovered at approximately 50 per cent (Stone 1980). However, this has since declined to less than 20 per cent in 2002.

The facts are similarly revealing when you look at the number of groups and branches that were present prior to 1980, compared to the number of talk shows. Prior to 1980, for instance, the PNP had approximately three thousand active groups. Simultaneously, there were only two talk shows on the island. This figure changed significantly by 2004, with less than two thousand active groups in the PNP and more than fifteen talk shows on different radio stations, with a cumulative listenership of more than one million.

The growth of talk shows has resulted in increased criticism and distrust for political authorities. Citizens are demanding greater accountability and transparency in government, and the format has intensified public scrutiny of political actors. This has contributed to high levels of distrust of politicians among citizens, as well as more corrupt practices in government being exposed, which has led to a high level of apathy about the political process. In 2002, for instance, approximately 41 per cent of the voting population stayed away from the polls, and while this is a part of a global phenomenon, it nevertheless constitutes an all-time high for Jamaica (ECJ 2002). Therefore, it can be argued that while the media has contributed to the broadening of democratic participation by providing more avenues for political dialogue, it has also contributed to the greater independence of Jamaicans from their leaders and political organizations, as well as the reduction of citizen voting in national elections.

The expansion of the media, especially in radio and cable television, has led to the development of niche marketing – radio and cable productions for specific audiences. According to Brown (1998, 52):

> Inevitably, a direct consequence of government liberalisation policies has been market segmentation by broadcasters. New players quickly recognized that gaining market share from the established players meant providing alternative or specialized programming to listeners as well as targeting specific audience segments. Whereas previously, broadcasters designed their programming for general audiences, today there is specialized or niche programming. All-reggae, all-calypso, all-Indian music, adult contemporary and religious programming is the norm rather than the exception in this competitive broadcasting environment.

The broadening of the media landscape, coupled with improvements in modern technology and niche marketing, has contributed to an explosion of the dance-hall culture, and it also has served to intensify its popularity through live broadcast of parties, stage shows and other venues for music. Irie FM, for example, a local radio station, is involved solely in the promotion of reggae, while Hype TV, a local cable channel, is prepared to take their viewers to the dance hall, live and direct.

Youths are the major source of influence on this music, and it has also affected the way they think and act (Hope 2013). Young people now view celebrities and superstars as their authority figures, and as a result, they show greater respect towards them than towards politicians.

Ownership

The issue of ownership of the media has not escaped the liberalization process. Previously, the government was the dominant player in the industry, owning the sole television station (JBC TV), two radio stations (JBC Radios One and Two) and the Jamaica Information Service (JIS), as well as having a 15 per cent interest in the sole private radio station, RJR. All of this changed when additional licences were granted to new players in the industry in the 1990s.

But with the introduction of these licences, the elites of the society have consolidated their hold on a large segment of the media landscape. For example, up to 2016, the two major daily newspapers were owned and operated by two of the wealthiest families in Jamaica: the Clarkes and the Stewarts. Now other elites are investing, such as Lee-Chin, who bought into CVM TV. This gave this family a controlling stake in one of the radio stations as well, as the station had acquired a licence to operate one and it also had control of the major cable station – FLOW.

Ownership of the media has implications for the shaping of public opinion and the formulation of decisions by governments based on the significant reach into a large segment of the population. Owners have the power to determine what the public views and reads on a daily basis – what Lippmann (2004) referred to as gate-keeping. In Jamaica, the two newspapers, for example, reach approximately five hundred thousand subscribers on a daily basis, and the cable company referenced has a subscription of approximately 750,000. Because these families have such a dominant stake in the media industry, with the power to determine what is broadcast, one can therefore understand their influence over the shaping of public opinion and influencing of government policies.

The relationship between political communication and political culture is organic. Understanding the political culture of a society is a necessary ingredient for effective communication. There is a clear and distinct political culture emanating from social institutions such as schools, churches, trade unions, political parties and the media within Jamaica. The political culture has been instrumental in the practice of political communication in the island. Political strategists and policymakers must understand this culture in order to develop effective communication strategies to correct some of the deficits identified.

The formation of groups and branches by the political parties in communities across the island was a deliberate act to aid the process of communication of their programmes and policies. The advent of electronic media, coupled with other endogenous factors such as limited financial resources on the part of the politicians, has contributed to the virtual emasculation of these groups and branches, which has negatively affected the depth of the country's democracy. The groups and branches were a buffer for the political parties in communities across the island, and with the advent of electronic media, they have become virtually nonexistent. Therefore, a vacuum has emerged between citizens and their leaders, which is manifested ultimately in apathy among voters.

The media is now leading and shaping the political dialogue on freedom and order in Jamaica. Indeed, they have become the pre-eminent socializing institution in the public sphere, using their influence to help citizens in making greater political and economic choices. This is compelling political figures to act in the public interest or else face the consequences of political and economic disaster.

Through the expansion of the media, there has been a broadening of democratic participation in Jamaica. This has manifested itself through the various talk shows that have proliferated throughout the country over the past twenty years. Citizens can call in to talk shows to express their opinions on issues and get responses to their concerns in real time. This proliferation of the media has undoubtedly contributed to greater independence of Jamaican voters, whose manifestation is apparent in the decline in grass-roots support for the major political parties and the increase in the level of listenership and viewership for diverse media in the country. This may seem to be a paradox, but democratic participation does not confine itself to involvement with political parties. Democratic participation requires a consistent responsiveness to the preferences of citizens (Dahl 1971). Wherever reactions are seemingly positive, citizens will be responsive, and participation is likely to increase. In the new dispensation of political communication, political parties and their leaders have been constrained by their inability to respond to citizens' needs, resulting in a shift in citizens' dependence on them (Buddan 2007). A change is taking place with patron-client relations. The media is emerging as a significant avenue through which citizens can receive a response to their needs, so they are reducing their support for political leaders and their parties.

In the context of political communication, a theoretical argument can thus be extrapolated from the Jamaican experience. Citizen participation and satisfaction in the democratic process will depend on the nature of the political culture, the relationship between leaders and citizens, and the extent to which leaders communicate policy changes to them. If leaders and their political parties are responsive to citizens and there is effective communication, participation and satisfaction will be high. Conversely, if the leaders and their political parties are unresponsive and communication is poor, participation and satisfaction will be low.

3.

The Structure of Political Communication in Jamaica

Systems Theory

To understand and analyse the structure of political communication in Jamaica, I adopted systems theory in an attempt to identify possible gaps. Systems theory, developed by the Austrian biologist Ludwig von Bertalanffy in the 1920s, eventually became part of the social sciences. Kuhn (1974) was largely responsible for its transfer to the assessment of social institutions. The study of systems generally follows two main approaches: cross-sectional and developmental. A cross-sectional approach deals with interactions between two systems; conversely, the developmental approach deals with the changes that occur in a system over time. Within most systems, there are generally subsystems which are evaluated using three approaches: holist, reductionist and functionalist.

Kuhn (1974, 12) maintained: "The holist approach examines the system as a complete functioning unit. The reductionist approach looks downward and examines the sub-systems within the system and the functionalist approach looks upward from the sub-system to determine the role it plays in the larger system."

This book adopts a holist approach, as the complete system established in the Jamaican society to transmit information to citizens, and examines citizens' feedback to their leaders.

According to Kuhn (1974, 154): "One common component of a system is that knowing about one part allows us to know something about the other parts. Systems can be either controlled (cybernetic) or uncontrolled. In controlled systems information is sensed, and changes are effected in response to the information." He referred to this as the *detector*, *selector*, and *effector* functions of the system.

The detector is concerned with the communication of information between systems. The selector is defined by the rules that the system uses to make decisions, and the effector is the means by which transactions are made between systems. Communication and transaction are the only intersystem interactions. *Communication* is the exchange of information, while *transaction* involves the exchange of matter or energy. All organizational and social interactions involve communication, transaction or both. Kuhn (1974, 156) stressed that the role of decisions is to move a system towards equilibrium, as "communication and transaction is [sic] the vehicle which transports that system to equilibrium".

The systems theory forms the context for a structuralist or functionalist approach towards analysis, which requires a detailed examination of the institutions or mechanisms established for the good governance of a society or organization (Giddens 1984).

The governmental apparatus in Jamaica is fashioned after the British system, with certain institutions or structures designed to make decisions and transmit them to citizens. In this book, the structures are presented in two categories – formal and informal. Formal structures are established by law (the constitution) in order for the government to use to make and communicate decisions, while informal structures are those institutions such as the media and political parties that transfer information to citizens.

Formal Structures

The Cabinet

Under the system in Jamaica, grounded in the constitution and relying on the traditions of Westminster, the leader of the winning political party in a national election is invited by the governor general to form the government. The prime minister then names the deliberative and policy implementation body known as the *cabinet,* members of which are selected from the victorious political organization (Ministry of Justice 1962). The cabinet is the major decision-making body concerning policy and gets its legitimacy from the constitution. The first of these in post-independence Jamaica was appointed by Prime Minister Alexander Bustamante in 1962.

In all cabinets, ministers are responsible for different portfolios, including the significant assignment of a minister to the responsibility for information. In any administration, the holder of this portfolio plays an indispensable role in disseminating decisions taken by the government. That person must have a lucid understanding of cabinet decisions, as incorrect interpretations can introduce "noise" into the transmission of information to the public.

Since the 1990s, it has become an established practice for the reigning government to host a press conference immediately, or no later than a few days, after the cabinet's deliberation to give an indication of the issues that were considered and the decisions taken (Press Association of Jamaica 2018). The information is synthesized and presented to the media for transmission to the public. It must be noted that this practice of a postcabinet press conference became a standard feature of the governance process in Jamaica after the collapse of communism.

The international community had embarked upon a new era of openness and transparency, and citizens were demanding these measures from their government, along with more information on the decisions taken. Accordingly, press conferences became a standard feature of the governance process. In most cases, they were held before decisions were tabled in Parliament – a practice which raised concerns among some political commentators about their validity.

The Parliament

The Constitution of Jamaica provides for a deliberative body known as the *Parliament*, comprising members who won their seats representing all political parties in elections. They discuss and make decisions that are pertinent to the good governance of the country (Ministry of Justice 1962). In the context of the Westminster system, there is a fusion of power between the executive (cabinet) and legislature (Parliament). In this merger, members of the executive have to be part of the legislature; therefore, all ministers of government are part of Parliament. The cabinet is responsible for driving both administrative and legislative matters, and decisions that it takes are relayed to Parliament through a series of government channels. The normal flow stems from the Office of the Prime Minister and the varied ministries to the Parliament. There is also a provision for members of Parliament to introduce matters from their constituents through what is known as a *Private Members Motion*. This provision gives every parliamentarian the opportunity to table and debate any matter that is related to his or her constituency (Standing Orders of the House of Representative).

All administrative and legislative actions to be taken or deliberated by Parliament are coordinated by the leader of government business, subject to consultation with the leader of opposition business. Such consultations are needed in order to set the agenda of Parliament and to ensure that there is equity in the deliberation of the issues.

There are two chambers in Parliament: the House of Representatives, with sixty-three elected members, and the Senate, which has twenty-one members appointed by the governor general upon recommendations from the prime minister and leader of the opposition (Munroe 2002). Both houses have the responsibility of debating, reviewing and approving all the laws of the land. It is in Parliament that laws, regulations and resolutions are rigorously debated, making it one of the most important established structures designed to foster dialogue and facilitate the political communication process. The public can participate in these discussions when legislation is laid in the Parliament and referred to a Joint Select Committee. This committee comprises individuals from the House of Representatives and the Senate, who work together to deliberate on the intricacies of a particular piece of legislation. Sometimes a Select Committee is established, in which members of only one of the Houses of Parliament are chosen to deliberate on a particular matter.

There are ten Sessional Committees of the Parliament. These are recognized by Standing Orders, which govern the rules and proceedings of the Parliament, and they are allowed to run from session to session (Standing Orders of the House of Representatives). Since 1991, the committees of Parliament have been opened up to the media so that they can record the discussions taking place on public issues. Prior to 1991, all committees of the Parliament were closed to the media, and the public's business was conducted in the shadows.

Citizens are allowed to participate in the parliamentary dialogue either via writing to the chairman of a committee or the clerk of the Houses of Parliament, or by making a verbal presentation to the committee during meetings. The challenge is that most citizens are unaware of these opportunities for participation. Some citizens are also intimidated by the strict dress code established for attending parliamentary hearings or proceedings. Men are required to wear jacket and tie and women are expected to wear formal and modest attire. Given these restrictions and limitations, citizens resort to obtaining parliamentary information through the media, which is also a restrictive process. In most instances, the media fails to record the full discussions in Parliament, which has an impact on how the message is communicated to and interpreted by citizens.

Each year, the ceremonial opening of Parliament is characterized by the Throne Speech, delivered by the governor general. The speech, which generally highlights the government's legislative and administrative directions for the parliamentary year which runs from 1 April to 31 March, is delivered before a packed audience and under the bright spotlight of the media. A limited number of privileged members of the public, often from the elite, are granted the opportunity to sit inside the Parliament chamber to watch the proceedings. Uniquely positioned, they obtain a first-hand view of the programmes and policies to be implemented by the government for the legislative year.

A major instrument of communicating programmes and policies to citizens is the budget, the annual statement of revenue and expenditure, which comes after the Throne Speech and is debated in the Parliament. It highlights the estimated revenue to be collected by the government and the amount of money it will spend. The paramount presentation comes from the minister of finance, who opens and closes the debate. In the preliberalization period – that is, before 1991 (Brown 1998) – all members of the cabinet were required to make a presentation. However, there has been a sense of disengagement and disinterest by citizens since then, and as the media became liberalized, government no longer had control over what was broadcast on national television and radio. Consequently, Parliament had to make adjustments, so it opted to designate a shorter period and require input only from senior ministers of the government and spokespersons from Her Majesty's Opposition (the largest political party out of power). However, the sectorial debates were introduced, in which all parliamentarians could participate.

A central feature of the annual parliamentary debate is the presentation from the prime minister. It is important because it generally gives an outline as to the compendium of programmes and policies to be implemented by the government during that particular financial year. It is generally characterized by a response to some of the major developments taking place in the country. Successive prime ministers have used this speech to announce a number of social and financial benefits – "goodies" – for citizens.

For contributions of the prime minister and the leader of the opposition, full mobilization generally takes place. This happens on two fronts: the mobilization of supporters loyal to the political parties and the full attendance of the electronic and print media. These are significant because the presentations by these two leaders constitute a single major national speech, as political parties and their parliamentary representatives want to ensure that their leaders' messages are communicated directly to citizens. The media, especially radio and television, is used to transmit these speeches to a broader audience in real time.

There is an observation that must be made from a political communication perspective with regard to Parliament. It is in this institution that the fundamental philosophy behind political communication is consistently manifested. Both political parties that have dominated Parliament since the 1960s have clearly identified themselves with one side or the other of the debate driving political communication: the PNP on the liberal side (freedom) and the JLP on the conservative side (order). The speeches delivered by the leaders, especially during the budget debates, are generally framed from these two perspectives to send signals to citizens who identify with their political viewpoints.

The Ministries

Ministries are headed by cabinet members called *ministers*, who are responsible for specific subject areas. Each minister has support staff, headed by a permanent secretary who is responsible for administrative functions.

The public relations officer, who coordinates all media-related activities, is an important member of the support staff, through whom all information from the ministry is prepared, packaged and disseminated through the media to the public. This person is also responsible for gathering critical feedback on the varied programmes and policies being implemented by the particular ministry.

Informal Structures

The Government Media Service

Ever since electronic media was introduced to Jamaica (starting with radio in 1949), administrations have sought to control the manner in which information is packaged and released to the public. In 1962, the JBC was established by the government. A year later, the sole television licence was granted to JBC TV (Dunn 2012), also under government control. The government had also added other sources of information, such as the Government Public Relations Office in 1956, which was later changed to the JIS in 1963.

This approach to the media and the transmission of information to the public by government came within a context of the philosophical view that government should control information and determine how it is disseminated. This view was largely upheld by administrations with a socialist perspective. The PNP, which formed the government in the 1950s (at around the same time electronic media was introduced in Jamaica), is a democratic socialist organization, which accounts for its adherence to this approach to the media and information. Ironically, its attitude changed in the 1990s, as it aggressively pursued the liberalization of the media due to a global shift which was taking place as countries across the world abandoned hard-line socialism and embraced the market as the means for managing their economies (Panton 1993).

The liberalization of the media in the early 1990s resulted in a crucial shift in the structure of government communications policy (Brown 1998). Government's dominance was significantly minimized, as it was left with the JIS as the major means for transmitting official state information. As a condition of the licence granted to private media companies, sixty minutes of daily broadcast time was reserved for the government to make information available to the public on their programmes and policies.

With the introduction of the Internet, the JIS expanded its reach to citizens, adding social media platforms to aid them in disseminating information. It uses Twitter, Facebook and YouTube, and to date, its website is the third most widely used in the country, with over forty thousand regular users (JIS 2011).

In 2006, the Government of Jamaica launched the Public Broadcasting Corporation of Jamaica, a cable station established to cover issues deemed extremely important to the public. Unlike the JIS, however, this station does not solely concentrate on information from the government; it covers a wide array of issues, including information from opposition political parties.

Political Parties

As discussed in chapter 2, political parties play an indispensable role in national development, establishing mechanisms and structures to relay information to citizens at the grass-roots level and to receive feedback on the implementation of national programmes and policies (JLP 2003; PNP 2008). Critical to these structures are the groups and branches located within communities island-wide, aimed at receiving and disseminating information from their leaders and relaying community information back to top leadership.

Groups and branches are supposed to provide feedback through the local divisional leadership and constituency committees. The constituency leadership has multiple organs through which to articulate feedback emanating from the groups and branches in the communities: the Regional Executive Council (PNP) and Area Council (JLP); the NEC (PNP) and Central Executive (JLP); and the Executive Committee (PNP) and Standing Committee (JLP). If these executive bodies fail to express the concerns coming from the communities, the groups and branches can articulate their concerns at the annual conference of the particular political organization (PNP 2008; JLP 2003).

As chapter 2 examines, however, the group and branch structures have been seriously debilitated and are now a mere shadow of what the founders of the political parties had anticipated. Consequently, citizens have become more and more dependent on information from the mainstream media, which are oftentimes not able to give the full details, constrained as they are by time (radio and television) or column inches (newspaper). This often contributes to the distortion of messages received by citizens. If an active group or branch existed, it would assist in correcting such distortions and seek further clarification or assistance from the leadership of its respective political organization.

The issue is further complicated when a political party is in government, as all of its human resources are devoted to governing the country. Generally this contributes to an abandonment of the basic structures of the political parties which are designed to facilitate good governance. The situation leads to disconnection between the governors and the governed and has contributed to the growing apathy that characterizes the Jamaican political process (Anderson 2015).

This apathy has consistently been revealed by polls. Those conducted by Stone, Bill Johnson and Don Anderson since 1989 have shown a consistent trend where between 20 and 40 per cent of the population are frustrated with the political process in Jamaica (Anderson 2015; Stone 1989a). A number of scholars have advanced various reasons for this. However, from a political communications perspective, the data shows some clear gaps in the way that leaders and citizens engage with each other, including the breakdown of the group and branch structure designed to facilitate community-based communication and dialogue.

Prior to 1989, interest and participation in the political process were high (Stone 1989b), as manifested in the voter turnout for elections. For example, in the 1976 and 1980 elections, approximately 80 per cent of eligible voters cast their ballots. Interestingly, the group and branch structures were extremely active at those times. In the PNP, for example, there were over three thousand active groups scattered in various communities. Similar data was unavailable for the JLP because according to Golding, the method for selecting delegates for the JLP changed in the 1970s, which had implications for the functionality of the branch network.

The presence of the media during that era was also less pronounced. Citizens had less access, as the high cost of radio and television sets meant that only a few people were able to purchase the necessary technology to retrieve information. Furthermore, the largely government-controlled media ensured that there was a specific way in which information was packaged and transmitted to citizens. Information flow was circular, moving from the leaders to the Parliament, to the media, to citizens, and back to the leaders. However, there was breakage in this flow.

Following the liberalization of the economy, more citizens gained access to the media, as there were now more ways to disseminate information to citizens and the cost of the needed equipment dropped, making it more affordable. Citizens became more dependent on the media for information, as they viewed media sources as more credible than those of the political organs. What the country had not seen, however, was simultaneous reform to the group and branch structure of the political parties. Here, it seemed, lay the main break in the flow of communication. As the groups or branches tasked with the responsibility of transmitting correct information in the communities and providing feedback to their political leaders faded, room was created for distortion and rumours to foment. Simultaneously, the absence of groups and branches made it difficult for leaders to have their supporters take their message directly to others on the ground, thus contributing to the ineffectiveness of that communication strategy. Group and branch networks, therefore, have to be reformed to make them more active in and responsive to the communities to improve the linkage between the governors and the governed.

Conclusion

Based on the systems theory, then, in the context of this volume, the *detector* is the media, because it deals with the communication of information from different structures in society. The *selector* is the cabinet, responsible for formulating the rules that are used to make decisions, and the *effector* is the public, because it deals with the transaction of information between the different systems. For the system to move towards equilibrium (that is, an efficient and effective flow of information between the governors and the governed), all components must operate efficiently. However, as we have argued and seen from the data, this is not the case in Jamaica. There are gaps in the structures that have been established to facilitate the smooth flow of information between the organs of the society.

It is clear from the structures that the cabinet is the pre-eminent decision-making body in the Jamaican political landscape, as it is here that policy is formulated and approved. However, periodically, it has taken decisions that have frustrated citizens because there was limited or no consultation with them. Habermas (1984), in his *Theory of Communicative Action*, argued that such action required some form of consensual decision on the part of the stakeholders in a particular action, while Blumler and Gurevitch (2001) noted that without consensus, there will be discontentment in the society.

Both JLP and PNP administrations have been guilty of this. For example, the Seaga JLP regime of the 1980s took certain economic decisions that led to the retrenchment of approximately six thousand civil service jobs. This decision formed part of an agreement with the IMF and World Bank to reduce government expenditures. Little or no consultation was done with citizens, however, this had negative political consequences for the Seaga administration and undoubtedly contributed to its defeat.

Then, in 1991, the Manley-led PNP took a decision to liberalize the economy. This was a major policy shift for the PNP, which had previously established itself as a democratic socialist organization. The decision led to subsidies being removed from certain basic food items, which had profound implications for the population, as the price of goods and services was now determined by the market. These decisions were taken with insufficient consultation with the general population and, more specifically, with the groups within the PNP, contributing to a significant disconnection between the PNP and the people.

These arguments will be explored further in subsequent chapters, but what must be highlighted here is that the lack of consultation and dialogue with grass-roots organizations undoubtedly hinders equilibrium in the communication process. Their exclusion from decision-making will only lead to frustration and when people are frustrated, they will abstain from the political process. This is what is occurring in the Jamaican political process today.

4.

Communicating Economic Programmes and Policies

The 1970s

In the 1970s, Jamaica experienced a shift in its pursuit of an economic strategy. Prime Minister Michael Manley and his regime felt that the economic model being implemented was generating economic growth but little employment, and this contributed to growing inequality within the society (Manley 1974). Consequently, in 1974, he reinstated democratic socialism as the philosophical underpinning of the PNP to drive the development of the economy and society (Panton 1993). During this period, the government played a lead role in the production of goods and services and the ownership of assets within the economy. The ownership of some of these properties admittedly came about due to capital flight, which emerged after the announcement of the philosophy and the close association that the regime developed with communist states such as Cuba and the Soviet Union (Stephens and Stephens 1986).

In the democratic socialist experiment, Manley rejected Sir Arthur Lewis's economic model of "industrialization by invitation", confronted the local oligarchy's dominance on the economy and challenged the owners of the bauxite industry (Stephens and Stephens 1986). Internationally, he denounced the global economic system, called for the establishment of a New International Economic Order and forged closer ties with like-minded countries of the global South such as Venezuela, Cuba and Libya, as well as with China and the Union of Soviet Socialist Republics (USSR). These relationships were known as *South-South cooperation* (Manley 1991).

But confronting the local and international status quo had serious consequences. Speaking to the *Multinational Monitor*, Manley (1980) stated:

> Jamaica has had a very firmly established, a historically established, oligarchy. It was a very elitist society; it really was not a society characterized by anything we would loosely call social justice. And we firmly addressed that issue. It had to be addressed; it was not negotiable in terms of our principles.
>
> We found that this led to a very hostile reaction by the people with money, the people from the entrepreneurial class, the landed people. I mention the last factor

because when the crunch came in 1973, an inner crunch came as well. That inner crunch came because this oligarchy largely took off, and took a tremendous amount of money out of the society. Now a lot of things that we've been accused of in terms of mismanagement really arose because, added to all the other shocks to the economy, the departure of these people really was a heck of an extra blow.

The exodus of large segments of the oligarchic class from Jamaica resulted in the state's greater involvement in the production of goods and services, leading to a decline in economic growth. This was further exacerbated by external shocks such as significant increases in the price of oil in 1974, which forced the government to enter into a borrowing relationship with the IMF in 1977. This signalled the commencement of Jamaica's debt problem (Stephens and Stephens 1986).

The first two years of the IMF relationship were problematic. Jamaica was required to make serious adjustments to its budgetary expenditure on critical areas of the economy, such as health and education. The country was also instructed to suppress wages and salaries for public-sector workers and to devalue its currency. These were part of the conditions imposed upon Jamaica if it wanted receive loans to deal with its balance of payment problems (Morris 2001). However, many scholars and individuals within the PNP felt that the IMF was being used as a means to curtail Jamaica's relationship with communist states, and this caused problems between the Manley regime and the IMF.

The IMF placed great emphasis on economic indicators and insisted on a reduction of government expenditure on social services. These and other prescriptions ran counter to the democratic socialist philosophy of the PNP and were strongly rejected by the party. Consequently, in 1979, a political decision was taken at an NEC meeting to terminate the borrowing relationship with the IMF (Morris 2001). According to the general secretary, D.K. Duncan, NEC members felt that the IMF's prescriptions were harming the progress of the society and if this continued, Jamaica would become an impoverished state.

Between 1979 and 1980, the issue of the economy and the economic model being pursued by the government was the subject of discussion in every sector of the society. Intense political dialogue emerged about the economic model being practised and whether it was appropriate for Jamaica. The public sphere was engulfed in a bitter debate over democratic socialism (PNP 1978) versus capitalism (Zimbalist, Sherman and Brown 1988), a reflection of the ongoing debate of "freedom" versus "order". So contentious was the debate that it engendered tribalized warfare between the two political parties, which resulted in the death of over eight hundred Jamaican citizens (Campbell 2014). The deaths undoubtedly contributed to a "toxification" of the political discourse in the country, ultimately contributing to a regime change in 1980 as the JLP, led by Seaga, defeated the PNP in the national elections (Panton 1993).

The 1980s

This decade once again saw a shift in the economic model being pursued by Jamaica. The Seaga-led government abandoned the democratic socialism of the Manley regime and returned the economy to capitalism. Essentially, the government accepted the international division of labour and economic order, aiming to have Jamaica "outcompete" other developing countries in reaping the potential benefits of investment by the industrialized countries (Seaga 2009).

One of the first decisions that Seaga took was to re-establish a borrowing relationship with the IMF. According to him, this was essential because all the possible resources of the country had been depleted and the IMF was the quickest way to obtain funds to jump-start the economy (Seaga 2009).

He also moved to re-establish a positive relationship with the governments of the United States and Britain and disconnected from those of Cuba and the Soviet Union. The ideological posturing was intended to reap tremendous benefits for his economic development plans. His regime received significant loan and grant funding from the US administration, led by President Ronald Reagan, through organizations such as the IMF, World Bank, the Inter-American Development Bank, the Caribbean Basin Initiative and the United States Agency for International Development.

It must be noted that the establishment of a relationship between the Seaga-led JLP and the Reagan-led Republican Party in the United States was no mere coincidence. Both leaders and their political parties shared the same philosophical perspective. Both supported order in the ongoing political dialogue and were members of the International Democratic Union, an umbrella organization of conservative political parties. This, therefore, provided an avenue for Seaga to gain the necessary financial and economic support from the Reagan administration (Seaga 2009).

Notwithstanding this fact, the loans and grants received from the US government and donor agencies were not to be obtained without certain conditions. A clear understanding was that the economy would be transformed to a market-driven, private sector–led enterprise (Stone 1989b).

The IMF in particular required that a number of conditions be met in order for the government to access their loan facilities. Through the IMF's stabilization programme, the government was required to curtail government spending and to build its foreign exchange reserves. Failure to meet the respective targets set by the IMF would result in the government not being able to access loans from donor agencies.

Conversely, the World Bank, through its Structural Adjustment Programme, required rigorous divestment and privatization of major government-owned assets and the rationalization of social services (Seaga 2010).

The IMF and the World Bank provided significant loans to the Seaga regime. In the *Multinational Monitor,* the journalist Fitzroy Nation (1984) penned: "Charting a strident free-enterprise course, the ruling Jamaica Labour Party has opened up the economy to foreign imports and has placed heavy reliance on the private sector to restore economic vibrancy by expanding exports. But it has encountered serious difficulties with the IMF, which agreed in April 1981 to support this program by providing a [US]$650 million loan over three years."

But Jamaica consistently failed to meet the various performance criteria outlined for that particular Extended Fund Facility, and the agreement had to be abandoned by 1983. It was subsequently replaced with a one-year credit arrangement with the IMF which included a call for the retrenchment of approximately six thousand jobs from the public sector (Nation 1984).

It was not long before the Seaga regime would find itself facing major problems as a result of implementing both the stabilization and structural adjustment programmes of the IMF and World Bank. The drastic measures had negative effects on the Jamaican people. For example, the retrenchment of six thousand public-sector workers based on the requirements of these institutions cut deep into the political culture that emerged in the society and caused extensive discomfort among citizens. By 1982, public opinion polls were showing the JLP trailing the PNP, and if elections had been called then, the Seaga administration would have been in serious political trouble (Stone 1982).

As pointed out in chapter 2, a patron-clientelistic culture had developed in the society, creating a dependency on politicians and the government apparatus, and the retrenchment jettisoned individuals from the establishment that would have formed part of this political culture. By the mid-1980s, the Seaga regime was having problems with the country's multilateral and bilateral institutions. Public opinion was that the government's programmes were not being implemented at a pace that would transform the economy. According to Seaga, this primarily had to do with the pace of privatization of some of the hotels owned by the government; but there were no recorded accounts of government-owned hotels through the Jamaica Hotel Holding Company. This posed a major problem for his administration when it came to disposing of these assets, much to the chagrin of the multilateral institutions (Seaga 2010).

Seaga had a number of confrontations with the leaders of these organizations. In his opinion, they were not being sympathetic to some of the issues facing the economy or, by extension, the Jamaican people. As a result, a fact-finding mission by a senior official of the IMF was sent to look at the socioeconomic issues in the country. According to Seaga, this never yielded anything – it only worsened the relationship between Jamaica and the IMF. Seaga continued to resist requests for the Jamaican currency to be devalued, and in 1985, he established a fixed exchange rate (Seaga 2010). This was after the country was operating under a floating exchange rate mechanism since 1980 and had seen the currency depreciate from J$2: US$1, to over J$4: US$1 – a decline of over 100 per cent in a four-year period. According to Seaga, the economy failed to respond to the treatment by the IMF, and this justified his resistance to the fund's regime (Seaga 2010).

The economy finally responded after the fixed exchange rate was established in the latter half of the 1980s. According to Seaga, the fixed exchange rate mechanism brought about greater stability in the foreign exchange market, and businesses were now able to plan more effectively. As a result, a number of projects came to fruition. The manufacturing sector in particular saw significant growth through investments in the 807 Garment Project and the opening of free zones. There was also growth in other areas, such as tourism, mining, construction and information technology. According to the Planning Institute of Jamaica (PIOJ 1989), the economy grew 5–6 per cent between 1985 and 1989.

Undoubtedly, the economic model pursued by the Seaga regime in the 1980s produced some results, especially later in the decade. For example, there was a stable exchange rate, low interest rates, low inflation and declining unemployment rates. However, the gains that were made on the economic side were affected by the cuts in government expenditures on some critical social programmes that were designed to assist citizens. This contributed to the defeat of the JLP by the PNP in the 1989 national elections (Stone 1989b).

The 1990s

The ascension of the PNP ushered in a new era of Jamaican politics. Michael Manley and his regime were once again put in charge with a popular mandate from the Jamaican people. This time, however, they took a different approach to the issue of economic development. The democratic socialist posture of the 1970s was significantly transformed, and prominence was given to the market-driven economy. According to Paul Robertson, general secretary of the PNP, under Manley's leadership, the party had undergone a series of internal discussions about this new approach through the groups, the regional councils, and the NEC and annual conferences. Moreover, by this time, the collapse of communism in the Soviet Union and other parts of Eastern Europe was well under way, so most of the countries that offered support to Manley's regime in the 1970s were themselves embracing change and adopting the market as the mechanism for distributing and producing goods and services.

On returning to office, Manley was faced with the daunting challenge of rebuilding and reconstructing an economy negatively affected by Hurricane Gilbert in 1988. In addition to significant deterioration of the social infrastructure, he had to deal with a growing debt problem that had ballooned during the previous Seaga regime. With Jamaica back into a borrowing relationship with the IMF, lingering memories of the experiences during the 1970s resurfaced. This time, however, Manley had no choice but to respond to the IMF's offerings.

The IMF and the World Bank were disappointed that the Seaga regime of the 1980s had failed to carry out a more comprehensive reform of the Jamaican economy. In fact, it was believed by some members of these two organizations, as well as the Reagan administration, that the Seaga regime had introduced state capitalism. Manley was therefore compelled to accelerate the modernization of the economy through a rigorous liberalization and privatization programme. This was done between 1989 and 1992, when Manley retired from national politics.

According to Meeks (1991, 4): "The new Manley/PNP government, in a manner not dissimilar to ideological shifts which would later lead to Bill Clinton's and Tony Blair's ascendancy, seemed to subscribe fully to the new paradigm. Manley on many occasions personally defended the efficacy of market relations and the government embarked on an energetic policy of privatization and import and currency liberalisation."
He further postulated:

> Manley defended his 1989 policies on the grounds that he had few available options in a new world order and, in an adverse situation, had sought to maintain key egalitarian components, including a program of worker participation, a push to spread ownership through the redistribution of shares to workers, the establishment of a "Micro Industry Development Agency" out of funds obtained from state privatization, to help the poor establish small businesses, and the resumption of the land reform programmes.

This liberalization of the economy by the Manley regime affected several areas of significance. It involved the floating of the exchange rate, so that its value was determined by the market; the removal of subsidies from a range of food items; and the freeing up of the motor vehicle industry. These were some of the areas that received immediate liberalization. On their effectiveness, comments by Kari Levitt in an exchange with Manley are worth considering (Levitt 1991, 4):

> I think it is now clear that the neo-liberal model has failed to deliver either stability or growth. Floating exchange rates and perpetual devaluations proved to be disastrous, and have mercifully been abandoned in favour of exchange rate stability. They failed to close the trade gap, which has now been aggravated by the reduction in duty on motor vehicles, and the encouragement of the importation of used cars, and is out of control. Last year, two-thirds of bank credit was allocated to consumption expenditures. The manufacturing industry is in decline, unable to compete with imports from higher-wage CARICOM [Caribbean Community] countries. Equipment is run down. Plants are closing. The "mopping up of liquidity" by issue of CDs has acted as an engine of redistribution from the poor to the rich . . . the model is not working. Perhaps it can work in other countries where political democracy was suspended for long periods of time – as in Chile. Be that as it may, it is not working in Jamaica.

Levitt (1991) and Meeks (1991) reflected some of the criticisms levied at the policies implemented by the new Manley regime after 1989. In 1992, Manley retired from national politics, and the baton was passed to Patterson, who continued with the policies of privatization and liberalization. However, he expressed his clear intention to move away from a borrowing relationship with the IMF as soon as possible.

One sector of the economy to benefit from the accelerated liberalization programmes was the media. A number of new radio stations and newspapers emerged. This development further accelerated under the Patterson administration as more television and cable stations began operations. This is of notable significance to this book because it marked the basis upon which the media became a paramount institution within Jamaican society, facilitating the growth of freedom of expression, free choice and access to information, and hence providing fertile ground for the practice of political communication.

But accelerated liberalization also brought significant hardship to most Jamaicans, especially the poor and vulnerable. For the first time, they were required to bear the full cost of most goods and services, at a time when the value of their income was diminishing. Inflation was spiralling out of control and the dollar was depreciating. There was a major contraction of governmental involvement in the economy, and the political actors (patrons and brokers) now had less to distribute to their supporters (clients).

Notwithstanding these hardships, the Patterson regime was able to secure another term in 1993. There were two major reasons for this. The first factor was the emergence of a new leader of the PNP and a new prime minister of Jamaica. There was the widespread view in the society that because it was the first time a black man had become the leader of the country, that he should be given a chance.

The second issue was related to the imbroglio that emerged in the JLP between its leader, Seaga, and a faction of Labourites who thought it was time he gave up leadership of the party. A feud ensued, and the organization became embroiled in political turmoil. Patterson immediately capitalized on the moment and called an election that resulted in the defeat of the JLP.

After the election, the Patterson administration had as one of its clear objectives stabilizing the economy, which had suffered from the aftershocks of liberalization. Inflation had skyrocketed due to devaluation and the removal of subsidies from major food items. The aim then was to contain inflation, stabilize the exchange rate and build the net international reserves (NIR), while simultaneously pressing for economic growth.

Another clear objective of the Patterson administration was to stimulate growth in the economy and to discontinue the borrowing relationship with the IMF. There was the continued view that the IMF's conditions were too stringent and were stifling the development of the country. In 1995, Patterson announced the end of this relationship. This time around, the decision was made on the basis of an improvement in the balance of payments and NIR position of the country, which indicated that there was no need for further support from that institution. This approach to the termination of the relationship with the IMF received great support from the Jamaican population for three major reasons:

- Citizens felt that this time, the decision was not made on the basis of mere politics, but rather on an improvement in the balance of payments position of the country.
- Citizens had by now borne the full brunt of the pressures brought about by the stringencies outlined by the IMF in its loan agreement with Jamaica and felt that it was time for it to end.
- The Patterson regime was in constant communication with the people through his "Live and Direct" presentations across the island. Information was readily available about the government's intention to end the borrowing relationship with the IMF and the basis for such a termination.

During the 1990s under the Patterson administration, economic stabilization was achieved, demonstrated by seven years of consistent single-digit inflation. The NIR had also grown to record levels. Between 2000 and 2005, foreign direct investment was averaging US$600 million (PIOJ 2006). However, the debt stock had increased to significant levels, and economic growth was anaemic. Notwithstanding, poverty levels fell from approximately 32 per cent in 1989 to 16 per cent in 2004 (PIOJ 2006). This improvement was largely attributed to some of the social programmes that the government had implemented to protect the poor and most vulnerable. These social programmes will be examined more closely in the next chapter, as the situation constitutes a paradox in the economic debate. There had been only anaemic growth in the economy during the period, which could not support the level of poverty reduction that the country had experienced up to 2006.

Admittedly, progress had been made to modernize Jamaica's economy under the PNP administration between 1989 and 2005. Through a rigorous programme of privatization and economic liberalization, Jamaica could be classified as having a market-driven economy with normal competition. It can be argued from the cases cited earlier, therefore, that up to 2005, the PNP administration enjoyed greater success transforming to a market-driven economy than the JLP had in the 1980s.

One can conclude the following from the qualitative descriptions:

- A market economy in which the prices of goods and services are determined by demand and supply has been the dominant means of managing the economy during the period under study. The transition for this process took place over time and culminated with full liberalization during the 1990s.
- The attainment of a market-driven economy was achieved through a number of policy combinations that came about through the stabilization programme of the IMF and the structural adjustment programme of the World Bank. Both programmes involved divesting from and privatizing government-owned assets, cutting off government expenditure and providing for the full liberalization of the economy.

Communication

The economic model dominantly pursued in modern Jamaica is quite clear. But to determine citizens' awareness of the version pursued by different administrations in modern times (1972–2006), we must find out whether there was a clear communication strategy to sell the model to citizens. In this context, we must examine the period when the market economy became a dominant force in Jamaican society, and thus highlight and analyse specific cases.

The Jamaica Labour Party

In an interview with Seaga, he emphatically stated that poor communication was one of the main factors contributing to the demise of his administration. According to him, this issue was treated in a cavalier manner, and even though there was a minister with responsibility for the information portfolio, there was no clear communication strategy. Information dissemination was confined to press releases, press conferences and public statements. It is clear that such approaches to communicating the programmes and policies of an administration would be woefully inadequate.

Seaga further lamented that because the attitude to communication was so poor, the gains of his administration in transforming the Jamaican economy and generating economic growth, especially in the mid- to late-1980s, were not sold to Jamaican citizens. According to him, this contributed to the defeat of his administration in 1989. This view was corroborated by Golding, who was general secretary of the JLP and minister of construction during that period. According to him, the communication strategy of the JLP administration during the 1980s was "abysmal".

But the failure of structures to strategically market the programmes and policies of the Seaga regime was not the only example of poor communication by that administration. Chapters 2 and 3 examined the structures of the political parties in Jamaica. Mechanisms were available to the Seaga government for communicating its programmes and policies to at least its base supporters through its branches and other organs. However, this never took place, and grass-roots members of the party had very little to do with the formulation of the programmes and policies that were being implemented.

This was a significant problem for the JLP. From its inception, the organization had a political culture that was leader-centric. Major activities and communication of policies were generally rotated around its leader. In the 1980s, this manifested itself in a fundamental way. According to Golding, the structures of the organization went to sleep while the JLP was governing. It therefore had difficulty having its grass-roots supporters carry the message of the government and provide critical feedback to the hierarchy.

A case-by-case examination of some of the economic decisions of the JLP administration will justify and validate my own conclusions, as well as those of Seaga.

THE EXCHANGE RATE

In 1985, Seaga's administration decided to move away from a floating exchange rate and return to a fixed exchange rate. This was contrary to the advice of the IMF and World Bank, as they deemed it to be against the principles of a market economy. The Manley regime of the 1970s had operated a fixed exchange mechanism with periodic devaluation, as prescribed by the IMF. In this mechanism by Seaga, the exchange rate would again be fixed and subject to periodic adjustment in order to facilitate Jamaica's competitiveness on the international market. According to Seaga, this change caused the economy to take off significantly, resulting in robust growth. Figures from the Planning Institute of Jamaica (PIOJ 1988) pointed to growth of between 5 and 6 per cent during the latter half of the 1980s.

However, this growth never resonated with Jamaicans – they voted against the Seaga regime during the very period when the economy was recording growth. According to Stone (1989b), citizens opted for politics over economics because the PNP was more strident with their marketing and communication strategies than the JLP. Each time there was an adjustment (devaluation) of the Jamaican currency, the opposing PNP would blame it on the Seaga administration and link it to increases in the prices of goods and services. The PNP did this through a series of economic fora conducted across the island, as they had no parliamentary status as a result of their boycott of the 1983 election. The regime failed to counter the PNP strategy, and one of the reasons, with which Golding agreed in an interview, was that the JLP structures were not functioning effectively.

AGRO 21

Another vital economic decision of the Seaga administration was the establishment of the Agro 21 project. Agricultural production was declining at the end of the 1970s. The sector was strategically important to the country because of its potential for foreign earnings and to generate employment. However, new strategies had to be found to modernize the means by which crops were produced. This project, therefore, was designed to transform the agricultural sector through the production of winter vegetables and other viable agricultural crops. Large commercial farmers were mobilized to export agricultural crops to the international market. They were linked to small farmers all over the island and created a network which would increase agricultural production for both the export and local markets. At the heart of this effort was the Spring Plains project, which was established in Clarendon. A farm in this area of Jamaica was designed with modern facilities that would contribute to the growth and production of winter vegetables that could supply the local and international markets. According to Seaga (2008, 1):

> In 1983, Agro 21 was launched. One of its objectives was to replace imports by growing food staples: corn, sorghum, cassava for animal feed, and rice and soya for human consumption. The rationale then was that with depreciation of the Jamaican dollar, which was a policy initiative of the Structural Adjustment Programme funded by the World Bank, the cost of production in Jamaica should be low enough to compete with imports. It was not. Local production costs were still too high, although sorghum came close to being feasible.

The initial experience with the Agro 21 project forced the regime to change course (Seaga 2008, 2):

> With the potential for growing crops for import substitution showing a lack of feasibility in the 1980s, Agro 21 switched to three other objectives: utilization of idle land, employment of idle hands and savings or earnings of foreign exchange . . .
>
> [According to a report submitted by the Planning Institute of Jamaica in 1988, the three objectives were highly successful]:
>
> Fifty thousand of a targeted 60,000 acres of idle lands were put into production, a 78-per-cent achievement; Twenty-six thousand, seven hundred and fifty new jobs for idle hands were created compared to a targeted 33,645, an 80-per-cent achievement; US$35.24 million of foreign exchange savings/earnings were recorded, a 69-per-cent achievement.

The Agro 21 project had the potential to transform the agricultural sector, create jobs and increase production in the country. It had the potential of affecting over one hundred thousand small farmers, whose economic existence was solely dependent on farming. But the Seaga administration once again failed to communicate its successes to the Jamaican people and instead allowed the PNP to use the negatives associated with the project to sway people away from the JLP.

But the PNP was not the only one critical of this agricultural initiative. Writing a report for the Heritage Foundation, a conservative think tank in the United States in 1986, Timothy Ashby expressed that country's disappointment with some of the policy initiatives as well. Seaga's own conservative colleagues were disappointed in the fact that instead of the JLP-led administration getting out of production, they were continuing to be involved through some of the programmes and policies they were promoting (Ashby 1986).

DIVESTMENT

The divestment of state assets was another major economic policy change by the Seaga-led administration in the 1980s. The Manley administration had had control of major assets within the economy based on a deliberate policy decision that the government would strategically own certain assets, as well as the result of the capital flight instigated by private individuals in the 1970s. Now, according to Seaga, fundamental decisions had to be taken to jump-start the economy: "The country had no money and so we had to divest those assets that could be divested in order to receive cash to do some of the things that we had to do."

He said that one of the vital divestments was the selling of shares in the National Commercial Bank, which since 1977 had been under government control. Shares were sold to ordinary citizens, causing them to become shareholders in one of the most powerful banks in the country (Edward Seaga, personal communication). It is estimated that approximately two hundred thousand ordinary Jamaicans were able to own, some of the shares in this company in 1986, but notwithstanding, the JLP led by Seaga was unable to transform this major achievement into electoral votes. Again, this spoke to a serious communication deficit by his administration in the 1980s. The PNP administration adopted a totally different approach in the 1990s. According to Seaga, he gave the PNP administration a "maximum" rating for their approach.

The People's National Party

Manley and the PNP returned to office in 1989, but this time under a reformed agenda. The democratic socialist rhetoric of the 1970s was revised and a new approach to governance adopted. This came at a time when the world was undergoing extensive political changes. Manley and the PNP also undertook some evaluation of their stewardship of the 1970s, and based on the consultations that were done among its members through the group structures, a decision was taken to adopt a new approach to governance. This new approach, documented in the *Compass,* would see the PNP embrace a plethora of more market-oriented policies in 1989.

In analysing the differences with the JLP in the approach to communication, we will focus on three economic decisions that were taken and how they were communicated to the public.

THE EXCHANGE RATE

The Manley regime recognized that to win the confidence of the private sector and to banish the experience of the 1970s, immediate action had to be taken to demonstrate the regime's commitment to market principles. One of the policies implemented in the early stages of the new Manley regime was that of a floating exchange rate. The previous Seaga administration operated a fixed exchange rate, and some private-sector operatives and the multilateral institutions argued that this was responsible for stifling the Jamaican economy.

Under this fixed exchange rate regime, individuals had to apply to banks for needed foreign currency. There was a considerable currency shortage, as exports were not earning enough to cover expenses for raw materials and other items needed for production. Members of the private sector and the multilateral and bilateral institutions believed that if the currency was liberalized and allowed to find its true market value, it would make Jamaican goods cheaper on the international market, and this in turn would induce greater demand for Jamaican goods and services.

In January 1990, the Manley regime devalued the Jamaican currency. However, by September 1991, a liberalized regime was put in place, and the Jamaican dollar was allowed to float to find its "true" value. This triggered a major depreciation of the Jamaican currency and contributed to disquiet in the society. The problem escalated because there were no funds in the NIR to back the local currency.

SUBSIDIES

Another major economic decision taken by the Manley regime between 1989 and 1992 was to remove subsidies from basic food items. This was a part of the programme of the IMF and multilateral institutions which wanted the government to reduce its expenditure so that it could pay its debt and deal with the balance of payment problem confronting the country. Up to 1991, the prices of basic goods were subsidized. Items attracting subsidies included sugar, rice, flour, skim milk, sardines and chicken-backs. Most, if not all, of these goods were produced overseas, and it was felt that this measure was subsidizing overseas producers.

But the removal of subsidies would bring about tremendous hardship on the poor and most vulnerable in the Jamaican society. It is estimated that over one million Jamaicans were negatively affected by this decision, announced by Seymour Mullings, minister of finance, in his 1991 budget presentation.

TRANSPORTATION

Upon assuming office in 1989, the Manley regime confronted a major challenge with public transportation, as the current system was inefficient and caused hardship on citizens. Manley was required to introduce new policy prescriptions to remedy this problem; the result was the liberalization of the motor vehicle industry.

Up until 1990, the importation of motor vehicles was done through the Jamaica Commodity Trading Company Limited. This company, which was government owned and operated, would sell motor vehicles to various car dealers on the island. They stood in long waiting lines for vehicles, as the government never had money to make purchases on a timely basis. This backlog in the demand caused public disquiet, so in 1990, the Manley regime decided to liberalize the industry and allow local individuals to import motor vehicles directly.

This decision received tremendous support from the private sector and the broader population. The private sector saw the new policy as a means of satisfying the high demand for motor vehicles and contributing to increased profits. Correspondingly, citizens saw this as an opportunity to own their own vehicles and lessen their dependence on the unreliable public transportation system. However, the move received opposition from the Seaga-led JLP, as they were concerned that this would strain the demand for foreign currency and contribute to the further devaluation of the Jamaican currency.

Manley/Patterson Approaches

While Manley was introducing these economic policy changes, he constantly used the media and the formal and informal structures available to his administration to update the nation about events. For example, he was noted for being a very good public orator. He used this skill to lead various parliamentary debates on the policies being introduced, and he also employed regular television broadcasts to communicate these policy combinations to citizens.

In 1992, increasingly ill health was affecting Manley's ability to execute his duties as prime minister, so he retired from politics. He handed the reins of government over to Patterson, who had emerged victorious in the PNP leadership race in February that same year.

Patterson explicitly emphasized that communication with citizens was a major priority for him and his administration. According to him, when he assumed responsibility for the Ministry of Industry, Tourism and Foreign Trade in 1972, Sir Edgerton Richardson, then financial secretary, advised him that for any administration to succeed, it had to be in constant communication and dialogue with the people. This advice was indelibly etched in his mind when he took over in 1992 as prime minister; communication with the people was critical, thus the introduction of the program called Live and Direct (Patterson 2018).

This was a mechanism to communicate programmes and policies of his administration to citizens in villages and towns across the country. Concurrently, there was the Face-to-Face programme, which was designed for members of Parliament to interface with their constituents on a regular basis about matters pertinent to their constituencies and the nation. Both of these initiatives took on the format of a town hall meeting, at which the prime minister or another minister would address the audience then entertain questions and answer them. According to Patterson, these two approaches to communicating with the people were responsible for his successful relaying of vital information to citizens at the grass-roots level.

Patterson further confirmed that the National Industrial Plan, which clearly outlined his administration's economic and industrial blueprint, had a lucid communication strategy. As a part of his general effort to communicate with the people, distinct aspects of the plan were articulated to citizens whether through Live and Direct or through Parliament.

A parliament is a major institution in the administration of any modern democratic society. As the PNP assumed office in 1989, citizens were being turned off by politics and what was taking place in the overall decision-making process of the country. The new PNP regime took the decision to open up several committees of Parliament to make the workings of this vital institution more transparent and visible to the public. According to Patterson, prior to 1990, none of the committees of the house were accessible to the general public, and information relating to the people's business was not readily available to them.

In Parliament, several ministry papers and statements by ministers were now being presented on a consistent basis. Parliament, Patterson notes, is the constitutional mechanism designed for those entrusted with the authority to communicate with the people. This is why the decision to terminate the borrowing relationship with the IMF was first announced in Parliament in 1994. This was a quintessential economic decision and the announcement constituted an unequivocal departure from the PNP of the 1970s, where a similar announcement was made at an NEC meeting in Ocho Rios, on the north coast of Jamaica. At that time, the public never bought into the decision, as it was strongly perceived as being political, not principled. Using the established constitutional mechanism to communicate the decision to end the borrowing relationship with the IMF in 1994 was received with greater enthusiasm.

Separate and apart from the procedural approach to communicating this vital economic decision by the Patterson administration, there were two factors that contributed to the enthusiastic response by citizens:

- The ideological rhetoric that had clouded the relationship between the PNP government and the IMF in the 1970s was now over, as communism had collapsed five years earlier.
- There was now a strong perception that the IMF was responsible for much of the hardship being faced by Jamaicans. Jamaicans arrived at this conclusion after witnessing multiple negative encounters that the Seaga, Manley and Patterson administrations had with the IMF. They had seen the increases in prices and the suppression of their wages, felt the effects on their lives, and linked all of this to the IMF. Therefore, the decision to leave the IMF in 1994 was construed as a welcome relief.

Another notable economic decision that the Patterson administration had to grapple with was the economic model being pursued. This was a pre-eminent issue for his administration because the Seaga-led opposition rejected the approach whereby the economy would be stabilized through the use of certain macroeconomic policies. This included low inflation, a stable exchange rate and an increase in the NIR.

Patterson observed that the model yielded a great deal of success even though the levels of recorded growth were lower than had been projected. Nevertheless, he argued, "There were seven years of consecutive single-digit inflation, significant increases in the NIR and consistent increases in FDI [foreign direct investments]" (P.J. Patterson, personal communication). Admittedly, Seaga and the opposition JLP disagreed. It was their belief that the model contributed to the growth of the debt stock and placed pressure on the exchange rate. They felt that this led to a number of complications in the economy such as the collapse of the financial sector in the mid-1990s.

This turned out to be another considerable economic issue for Patterson in the mid-1990s, as an estimated J$50 billion disappeared from the financial sector. The administration was faced with the horrendous task of rescuing it, because it had social as well as hard economic consequences and it is estimated that over one million Jamaicans would have been seriously dislocated as a result of the meltdown. In doing so, however, the administration had to explain to the people the rationale for intervening, as some felt that the government was bailing out its friends. Here again, Patterson was forced to rely on his communication strategy of Live and Direct. He was forced to once again address the matter and explain the rationale of the decision. Several Live and Direct and Face-to-Face discussions were held across the island to explain this particular issue.

Patterson also utilized the structures within the PNP to explain what had taken place with the collapse of the financial sector. Special speaker's guides were circulated through the NEC, regional executive committees, constituency executives, divisional executives and the groups within the organization, outlining what was taking place and what had led to the creation of the Financial Sector Adjustment Company (FINSAC).

Once again, the strategies paid dividends – although the collapse of the financial sector was a pre-eminent issue, the administration was given another mandate to continue to govern the affairs of the country after winning the 1997 national elections. The arguments of the Seaga-led JLP were severely discounted during this election campaign when it was discovered that Seaga himself was a major recipient of an enterprise loan from one of the collapsed banks. It was alleged that the loan was not being serviced, and that contributed to the bank's recurring problems. It therefore created a credibility issue for the JLP's communications strategy, and the Patterson-led PNP successfully used this in its campaigning.

In 1998, the Patterson administration made another decision that profoundly affected economic development. The liberalization of the telecommunications sector was a matter that would have positive consequences for the modernizing of the economy. Fundamental changes had to be made in this area for Jamaica to become a successful competitor in the global economy. The country also had to carve a niche in the global space as a significant service economy, and for this to transpire, the Patterson administration took the decision to break up the monopoly of Cable and Wireless Jamaica, then the sole provider of telephone services.

This was a daunting task. The company had been granted a fifty-year licence by the Seaga administration in 1988, so delicate negotiations had to be conducted and new legislation governing the sector had to be established. All of this was described in a ministry paper tabled in Parliament by the then minister of science, commerce and technology, Phillip Paulwell, which outlined the Patterson administration's new policy trajectory for telecommunications. In 1999, the government signed a historic agreement with Cable and Wireless, paving the way for the liberalization of the industry and the start of a new era.

Tremendous growth ensued in the sector as more companies entered the market. By 2000, the government had successfully auctioned off two cellular licences, which resulted in two new players: Cellular One Caribbean and Digicel. Cellular One Caribbean emerged the winner of the auction in December 1999 with a bid of US$45 million for the 800-MHz band using code-division multiple access (CDMA) technology. This bid was US$5 million more than the government's reserved price. In 2002, the majority shares in Cellular One Caribbean were purchased by Centennial Corporation, and Centennial Jamaica became Jamaica's CDMA telecommunications provider. Also in January 2000, Digicel won the auction for the GSM licence, with a bid of US$47.5 million. These two licences brought in a cumulative US$92.5 million within the first year of the new liberalized telecommunications regime.

The liberalization also resulted in more Jamaicans having access to telecommunications services. For example, according to the Statistical Institute of Jamaica (STATIN) (2006), approximately 1.7 million Jamaicans had access to either land lines or cellular phones. This opened more opportunities for Jamaican citizens, who now had greater access to information through services such as the Internet. The liberalization proved beneficial for the Patterson administration and contributed to the victory of the PNP in the 2002 national elections. The issue figured prominently in the campaign, as members of the PNP presented this as a major achievement.

The PNP once again used its structures to communicate its achievements to the public. A document entitled *Solid Achievements* – in which the liberalization of the telecommunications industry was discussed at length – was circulated to members, who then used it as a speaker's guide in their respective communities.

The PNP also used the campaign theme "Log On to Progress" in the 2002 election. This was a direct reference to the achievements that were made that allowed the ordinary Jamaican to access telecommunications services. Recognizing the patron-clientelistic culture within the society, citizens recognized this as a direct benefit and were responsive to the message. The PNP was given a fourth consecutive term in office – the first time that a political party had accomplished the feat in Jamaica.

In summary, it is evident that communicating with citizens is a fundamental requirement for the success or failure of an administration. A clear and defined strategy has to be designed by leaders and their political organizations to market an administration's impending economic programmes and policies. Seaga suffered significantly from serious communication deficits. During his tenure, there were no clearly defined communication strategies. Even though he enjoyed success generating economic growth in the latter half of the 1980s, his poor communications skills proved harmful to him and his administration. The marketing of government programmes and policies was treated in a trivial manner and was left solely to the issuance of press releases and press conferences. Seaga has admitted that this was one of the major factors that contributed to the demise of his administration in the 1980s. Additionally, despite the country's demonstrated economic growth, poor communication prevented many citizens from identifying with it, nor did they feel it in the quality of their lives. This was reflected in the poverty index, which showed that at the end of 1988, approximately 32 per cent of Jamaicans were living below the poverty line (PIOJ 1989).

On its face, the Seaga administration appeared to engage in what Habermas (1984) regarded as "communicative action". This type of action requires a consensual relationship with citizens. There was no consensus surrounding the economic programmes highlighted in this chapter, and this was made more difficult in Jamaica's tribalized political environment. Politics is a strategic endeavour, and therefore "strategic communicative action" was required to bring about greater political fortune for the Seaga-led JLP.

There was also a credibility factor that contributed to the defeats that the JLP suffered in the 1990s. The allegation of an unpaid loan that Seaga took from a commercial bank, as well as the fact that individuals within his own political organization wanted to see him resign, created a credibility gap and resulted in multiple defeats for the party in the 1990s. These issues contributed to distortions in the arguments on freedom and order within Jamaican society. Citizens were turned off from the message of economic management by the

JLP, as there were too many contending issues to grapple with in that political organization. The internal strife, the departure of Golding and other important party functionaries and Seaga's personal financial problems dominated conversations in the public sphere and contributed to the distortion of JLP messages and to communication problems, which resulted in several defeats until 2002.

Conversely, the Patterson administration had a concerted approach to communication with Jamaican citizens. Through the Live and Direct and Face-to-Face mechanisms, they were able to communicate some of the most complex issues to ordinary Jamaican citizens. They also utilized the organizational structures of the PNP to act as conduits to release information on programmes and policies to members in communities islandwide. These methods were employed alongside the formal structure established by the constitution (Parliament) to communicate with citizens. This made them able to market the most complex economic programmes and policies to citizens well and contributed to the levels of success enjoyed at national elections. As an example of this, the collapse of the financial sector was a difficult economic matter to explain, and yet it was packaged and sold to citizens in an understandable but tactful manner.

Until the 2002 elections, the PNP was able to connect with the ongoing dialogue taking place on freedom versus order in the public sphere. The policies that they implemented were skewed towards enhancing economic freedom. Whether it was the liberalization of the telecommunication sector to provide approximately 1.7 million Jamaicans with telecommunication services or the rescuing of the financial sector to protect over one million small depositors, citizens felt that the Patterson regime had effectively enhanced and protected their economic freedoms.

The liberalization of the economy established a market economy for the first time in Jamaica. A clear individualistic-consumerist culture emerged as a result. Citizens glorified the attainment of used cars, cellular phones and other imported goods that were now at their disposal. These were economic tangibles that they could identify with, and hence connect with, the campaign messages of the PNP. Also, these economic goods were in sync with the patron-clientelistic culture that existed in the society. Evidently, the Patterson-led PNP was involved in strategic communicative action, with the marketing of the economic programmes uniquely and deliberately designed to bring about specific results.

There is a need to determine whether Jamaican citizens favour a market-driven economy. It is one of the major policy initiatives to have been implemented by the three leaders under study, and since the 1980s, it has been the major vehicle through which economic decisions have been made. Whether such an economic policy is deemed favourable or unfavourable by Jamaican citizens is linked to the communication strategy used by the different leaders, and this question will assist in determining the level of their participation in the political process.

From the arguments presented thus far, one could readily conclude that Jamaicans do indeed favour a market economy. However, from a political communication standpoint, the answer to this is not so simple. In a study conducted by Powell, Bourne and Waller (2007), it was discovered that 62.3 per cent of the respondents did not favour a market-driven economy, and only 29.8 per cent did. This seems paradoxical to the varied election outcomes of the 1990s when the market economy was fully implemented. The PNP had managed to win four consecutive elections, despite the anaemic economic growth that took place in this period. It, therefore, means that there were other factors at play which contributed to this feat.

What is evident is the viewpoint that anything can be marketed. Once there is an effective communication strategy, the most difficult decisions can be communicated to the targeted audience. This is steeped in a capitalistic consumerist culture which recognizes the individualistic nature of humanity. This philosophy posits the view that because humans are individualistic, given the opportunity, they will be forced to make rational choices once they perceive that they stand to benefit.

In the context of a market economy, if there are competing forces, an individual will make a choice in favour of the force that has caused that person to earn a benefit. This reasoning is applicable to the Jamaican context of the 1990s.

The liberalization of the Jamaican economy by the Manley and Patterson regimes in the 1990s brought the PNP and the JLP, respectively, closer to the capitalist ideology. One could hardly distinguish between the programmes and policies of these two competing forces. In a competitive political environment, these organizations sought to distinguish themselves: the Seaga-led JLP sought to do so by talking about better management of the economy (order), and the Patterson-led PNP did so by focusing on the modernization of the economy to provide more goods and services to citizens (freedom).

Utilizing the individualistic-consumerist philosophy, one can explain the success of the Patterson-led PNP over the Seaga-led JLP during the 1990s. Jamaican citizens had to contend with two similar political products in terms of their economic outlook and were forced to make rational choices. The Patterson-led PNP was seen as the organization that brought citizens the benefits of cars, cellular phones and other consumer items, and hence a majority chose the PNP in three consecutive elections (a first for any political party in the history of Jamaica).

Citizens identified with the strategic political communication message from the Patterson-led administration, whereas there were considerable challenges with the delivery of the message of the Seaga-led JLP. It must be noted, however, that by 2002, the JLP had narrowed the gap in the number of constituencies won in the previous national elections. There is an explanation for this situation, which will be highlighted in the next chapter, focusing on communicating programmes and policies related to the social agenda.

5.

Communicating Social Programmes and Policies

The decade of the 1970s constituted a transformational period in the social landscape of Jamaica. It was the period when the widest range of social programmes was implemented and large numbers of the population were brought into full recognition.

In the previous decade, the country had experienced economic growth ranging from 5 to 6 per cent. However, the quality of life for most Jamaicans was less than satisfactory. When he assumed office in 1972, Michael Manley faced significant social challenges. He claimed that the average Jamaican could not read or write and children were being denied educational opportunities on the basis of the marital status of their parents (Manley 1974). These were only some of the issues contributing to poor quality of life for a large segment of the population.

In 1973, the government spent J$73.1 million on education. At this time, there were 434,351 children enrolled at the primary level; at the secondary level, there were 53,331 students attending sixty junior secondary schools, and 30,301 went to secondary high schools. The College of Arts, Science and Technology (now the University of Technology, Jamaica School of Agriculture) and the teacher training colleges had 4,852 students all together. In that same year, the University of the West Indies, regarded as the foremost educational institution in the region, produced 542 graduates from all three campuses combined. That same year, seventy-five thousand students benefited from the government's school feeding programme. This constituted approximately 12 per cent of the total enrolment at the primary and secondary levels of the system. According to the Social and Economic Survey of Jamaica, there were between four hundred thousand and five hundred thousand functionally illiterate individuals, representing 40 to 50 per cent of the adult population (PIOJ 1973). These statistics indicate the depth of the challenge inherited by the Manley regime, which was forced to introduce some major legislation and implement far-reaching social programmes to transform the landscape. Four of these instances, described next, will illustrate the situation.

Status of Children

In 1976, the Manley regime repealed the Status of Children Act, commonly known as the "Bastardy Act". This legislation had been in place since the days of slavery and impeded the progress of a significant number of black Jamaicans. It governed the treatment of children who were born out of wedlock and, as they were deemed illegitimate, they were not provided with the same opportunities as those born in a matrimonial union. Children who were labelled "bastards" could not attend certain schools.

Its repeal saw more "ordinary" black Jamaicans entering traditional, prominent high schools such as Munroe College and Jamaica College. While the policy shift was criticized by segments of the upper echelons of Jamaican society, the initiative received tremendous grass-roots support. It was viewed as a step towards social justice, as it empowered the vast majority of those black Jamaicans who were engaged in common-law relationships. Manley, who was instrumental in the parliamentary debate, indicated that the legislation had corrected a wrong which had been embedded in Jamaican society for decades. Its passage strengthened the confidence of ordinary Jamaicans in Manley and his administration, and that contributed to their victory in the 1976 election.

Health Care

The level of development in the health-care sector is important to any democratic process, and this area received extensive policy and programmatic focus from the Manley administration. This is one sector on which the masses focus when making political judgments, and so the government's responsiveness to and investment in this sector are critical to maintaining power.

Prior to 1972, the sector was severely challenged, as there was an insufficient supply of medical professionals and inadequate government investment. There were 490 practising medical doctors, 1,473 registered nurses and 669 assistant nurses. Health indicators such as mortality and morbidity rates were alarming. Infant mortality stood at 26.2 per 1,000, while the death rate was 7.2 per 1,000. Concurrently, there were 4,632 beds in hospitals, at an average of 21.4 per 1,000 people.

Mental health is an important indicator of citizens' ability to cope with the pressures of life. In 1973, 147 patients from the only psychiatric hospital, Bellevue, died, and 4,770 were discharged. That year, the hospital had 843 outpatients.

The Manley regime took the decision to address the situation boldly, starting with the allocation of 8 per cent of the budget, J$37.7 million, for health care in 1973, which rose to J$79.47 million by 1976, and introducing free health programmes. The situation with medical personnel was still perplexing, however. There were now 390 doctors, representing a reduction of 100 (or 10.4 per cent) compared to 1973, with approximately 180 doctors having left the system between 1975 and 1976. The complement of nurses increased by 915 (or 62.1 per cent), to 2,388, bringing the ratio of nurses to population to 1:878, an improvement from 1973.

By 1976, attendance at the Bellevue health clinic stood at 4,319, with 109 new patients and 183 clinical sessions. At the health clinics throughout the country in 1976, medical officers held 8,445 sessions, in which they saw 801,212 patients – 175,820 of them being new patients. The mortality rate for 1976 stood at 14.671 per 1,000, and it was 14.157 in 1973; and the infant mortality rate was 12.29 per 1,000 in 1976, an improvement from 16.22 per 1,000 in 1973.

Government's increase in investment in the sector coupled with the free health programmes featured prominently in the election campaign. A substantial portion of the population benefited, which could explain why the administration enjoyed popular support despite the country experiencing economic difficulties. The indication is that health policies were having a positive effect on appreciative citizens who returned the Manley regime to power in the 1976 election.

Literacy

Upon the Manley-led PNP assuming office in 1972, literacy presented a considerable challenge for most Jamaicans who had difficulty reading and writing the official language – English. To address this problem, Manley established the Jamaica Movement for the Advancement of Literacy (JAMAL), a special programme which taught adult Jamaicans to read and write. Over ten thousand volunteers who had received educational opportunities taught in the programme and by 1976, there were over ninety-two thousand individuals registered in over two thousand JAMAL centres across the island. The ratio was approximately nine JAMAL students to one volunteer teacher in this special programme. By 1980, over two hundred thousand Jamaicans had benefited.

Free Education

Scholars argue that one of the most revolutionary social policies to have been implemented in Jamaica was the granting of universal free education by the Manley regime in 1973 (Panton 1993; Stephens and Stephens 1986). It was revolutionary because it opened frontiers for ordinary Jamaicans to access a critical developmental tool up to the tertiary level, where professional training helped in the process of social and economic citizen empowerment.

Manley understood the importance of education for the transformation of Jamaican lives. He was insistent that the PNP-led administration had to take radical steps to ensure access to the education system by ordinary citizens for whom, prior to 1972, tertiary education was a dream. Scholars from the lower echelons of the society who acquired a college education and were extremely brilliant would receive scholarships. Prior to 1973, the University of the West Indies was an institution only the privileged minority could attend.

The position on free education was the subject of discussion at the cabinet level of the Manley administration. However, it was decided that while such a policy was ideal, the country did not have the money to finance such an initiative at the time. Manley was not satisfied with the decision, and invoking prime ministerial privilege, he announced in Parliament in May 1973 that the PNP administration was going to introduce universal free education. He did this without informing the minister of finance and planning, David Coore, or the minister of education, Florizel Glasspole. According to Coore, he had been privy to the cabinet discussion, but totally unaware of Manley's intent to make the announcement that he did in Parliament.

Under this initiative, the government was now responsible for the total funding of the education system and students would receive free tuition up to the tertiary level, as well as free uniforms and lunches. This received widespread endorsement in the Jamaican society at the time, including from a former JLP minister of education, Edwin Allen, who temporarily crossed the floor of Parliament to offer special commendation to Manley upon hearing the announcement.

The many social programmes announced by the Manley administration, such as those described here, were well received by ordinary Jamaicans in the regime's first term (1972–1976). They radically transformed the country, but they also were viewed as necessary for the development of an egalitarian society.

In the communication of these programmes, Manley as the PNP leader and prime minister could be seen and heard leading public discussions in Parliament, on television and on radio. The PNP structures also conveyed the messages on imminent legislation, programmes and policies within their communities. Germane to the process was the PNP publishing and circulating these reports to members via a newspaper called the *Rising Sun*. Furthermore, the details were features of the election campaign and could be heard in PNP songs that year. The substance of the social initiatives, as well as the successful communication strategy, contributed to the Manley-led PNP being returned to power in the 1976 election.

The Jamaica Labour Party – Seaga

The 1980s presented several challenges for the social landscape of Jamaica. It came within the context of both the stabilization programme of the IMF and the structural adjustment programme of the World Bank. Because of certain conditions imposed by these institutions, the country was forced to reduce its expenditure on important social services. During the 1970s, the Manley regime had introduced a compendium of social programmes geared at improving the quality of life of the Jamaican people. However, during the 1980s, these programmes were significantly affected by the strictures of the multilateral institutions.

After assuming office in 1980, the Seaga administration had to contend with the economy going through a turbulent period, and the government had no choice but to resume the borrowing relationship with the IMF. This had certain consequences, one of which was to cut expenditures to balance the budget. This is a typical multilateral institutional prescription and oftentimes, it is social services that are most affected. It was no different in Jamaica. The government had to dispense with some vital social services to hospitals, schools, youth services and other areas, and that would have negative consequences for the regime as time progressed.

By 1982, this was quite evident. Public opinion polls published by Stone (1982) indicated that had an election been called, the administration would have been in trouble with the electorate (Stone 1984). By 1983, the fortunes shifted due to Seaga's posture on the US invasion of Grenada. This point will be further elaborated in chapter 6.

Despite the challenges faced during the 1980s, however, some social programmes were implemented, with a positive impact. Four of these programmes are highlighted next.

HEART

In 1982, the Seaga administration introduced the Human Employment and Resource Training (HEART) programme. This was to be a national training agency for youths who had completed high school without the necessary qualifications, and thus could not find employment. Seaga had expressed his frustration with the apprenticeship system of the 1950s, which he had encountered when he was conducting sociological research across Jamaica. Armed with the knowledge and experience gained in that process, he proposed a national training agency of the nature and magnitude of HEART to the PNP administration in 1979. The proposal was not accepted, though, because trade training centres were already in place, according to the PNP.

But later, in 1982, his administration seized the initiative and implemented the idea. The programme came into effect via the HEART Act, and it offered skills training to young people who had left school, in areas such as garment construction, auto mechanics, horticulture, agriculture, cosmetology, electrical installation and hospitality services. Seaga had no hesitation introducing this programme, and he funded it by introducing statutory deductions from employers of 3 per cent of payroll. The context was growing stresses within the economy which demanded a skilled and trained labour force to embrace some of the opportunities being generated in agriculture, construction and manufacturing. A modern facility that would train young people to take up these opportunities was necessary.

The first HEART institutions were established at Stony Hill and Hope Road. Stony Hill HEART provided training in commercial fields, while Hope Road focused on cosmetology. By 1989, four similar facilities were built throughout the country at Runaway Bay for hospitality, Ebony Park for agriculture, Portmore for building construction and Garmex for training in garment construction. Thousands of young people across the island received training through this exceptional institution, but as discussed in chapter 4, the communication machinery of the Seaga administration failed.

Even though HEART was a visible and extremely important training institution, the level of marketing required to ensure that the country identified with this excellent initiative to train young people was woefully lacking. This enterprise, therefore, did nothing to alleviate the difficulties the administration faced in reaching the youth population of Jamaica in the 1980s.

Food Stamps

Introduced in 1982, the Food Stamp programme came about because certain social indicators were pointing to a decline in health standards for individuals in the lower quintile of the population. Consequently a stipend was granted to the most vulnerable so they could buy food. Approximately three hundred thousand individuals, including people with disabilities, senior citizens and pregnant and lactating women were targeted. However, the programme was overtaken by greed, as individuals who were not deserving of the assistance received regular payments and deprived needy individuals of a benefit specifically designed for them. Despite these corrupt practices, this project constituted a good attempt by the Seaga administration to ease the burden of the poorest in society.

Relief for the Disabled

The United Nations declared 1981 the Year of the Disabled. In this context, and recognizing that people with disabilities were among the most vulnerable groups within the society, the Seaga administration introduced a mechanism to provide income tax relief for this group. The population of people with disabilities in Jamaica in 2011 was approximately four hundred thousand (WHO 2011), and while the Ministry of Labour and Social Security (2015) estimated that only 10 per cent of this population was employed, the gesture was a fundamental one. People with disabilities incur a number of expenses on a daily basis. They must possess funds to purchase adaptive aids to function effectively in society, as well as to allow them to obtain ongoing medical treatment. Against this background, the Income Tax Act was amended to facilitate exemption for members of this community. Again, Seaga and his administration failed to communicate this far-reaching social initiative to citizens, and thus they did not mobilize them to participate in the political process on their behalf.

ROSE

Towards the end of the 1980s, various categories of schools existed at the secondary level. In an effort to streamline and modernize the system, the Seaga administration introduced Re-organisation of Secondary Education (ROSE). This was funded by the World Bank and was designed to standardize these institutions and bring them on par with global standards within a particular time frame.

However, the JLP could not point to ROSE as a major achievement, as the reform process was not completed in time for the 1989 election campaign. Furthermore, the introduction of various structural adjustment programmes which had a negative effect on the education system discounted any possibility of the party making a credible case in this area. The nation also had not forgotten that the JLP had introduced a cess on tertiary education, which led to a national protest in 1985.

These four social programmes represented genuine efforts on the part of the Seaga administration to deal with some of the challenges confronting the vulnerable within the society. It is estimated that cumulatively, they touched the lives of over six hundred thousand people – approximately 20 per cent of the population. This is a significant bloc of Jamaicans. However, once again, the administration never maximized the benefits, failing to consistently promote these programmes, and thus it suffered the consequences when the JLP was defeated in the national polls in 1989. If the programmes had been properly marketed and communicated to citizens, the Seaga administration could have secured different electoral results.

The historical data has always shown the PNP administrations as being strong on social policies and weak on economics. The reverse is applicable for the JLP. This is largely attributed to the philosophical orientations of these two political organizations. It was pointed out that in the political arguments taking place in Jamaica, the PNP identified more with the preservation of freedom and therefore was classified among the "liberals". Conversely, the JLP identified more with order and was classified as "conservatives". Therefore, PNP-led administrations placed a greater emphasis on social programmes, while JLP-led administrations focused on economic management.

Patterson

In the 1990s, the Patterson administration introduced a number of social programmes and expanded some initiatives started by the JLP. However, there were major differences in the treatment and marketing of the programmes and policies they implemented or modernized. Four examples illustrate this point.

HEART-NTA

Upon assuming office in the 1990s, the PNP took the decision to continue the HEART programme, but with some adjustments. The Vocational Training Centres which had existed in the 1970s were closed by the JLP in the 1980s. The Patterson administration revamped and reopened them and then added them to HEART, creating the Human Employment and Resource Training Trust–National Training Agency (HEART-NTA). The new move gave greater focus to the training institution, which became a megatraining agency for secondary school-leavers who wanted a second chance.

Moreover, the institution was expanded, and there was a training facility in every parish. In addition, HEART-NTA joined forces with grass-roots organizations including churches, resulting in the institution becoming a household name. It continued to offer training in original core areas and expanded into a number of others under the new PNP administration. In all of this, some citizens forgot that it was the Seaga administration that had established HEART because the new entity, HEART-NTA, had a renewed focus and the government placed greater emphasis on marketing the institution to the Jamaican people.

PATH

Patterson also continued the Food Stamp programme, which had lasted for approximately ten years, before subsuming it under a new arrangement, the Programme of Advancement Through Health and Education (PATH). It was perceived that the Food Stamp and the diverse other social welfare programmes designed for the most vulnerable had outlived their usefulness. They were not sufficiently covering the requirements of the needy and manifested many administrative inefficiencies. Consequently, the Patterson administration undertook a major reform of the social safety net. Several social programmes were overhauled to ensure that they became more efficient and that the groups that they were intended to benefit received what was rightfully theirs.

PATH conflated three programmes: the Outdoor Poor Relief, Old Age and Incapacity Benefits and Food Stamps. Unlike other social assistance programmes where a direct grant was disbursed to recipients, PATH beneficiaries were required to participate in certain activities to qualify for continued assistance, such as having regular health checks and verifiable school attendance. This was designed specifically to break the intergenerational cycle of poverty through the focus on human capital development.

The mechanism for selecting beneficiaries also changed. In light of limited resources, there was the need to target individuals most in need of the assistance. The Ministry of Labour and Social Security had this responsibility, and its staff went into communities to do mass registration. A scoring formula – the Beneficiary Identification System – was developed to ensure objectivity for selection. Over seven hundred thousand individuals applied for the available two hundred and thirty-six thousand spaces in the programme.

PATH was officially launched, with significant fanfare, in 2002 by Prime Minister Patterson at a special function in one of the rural constituencies (North West St Catherine). Intense advertisement followed in the media. It must be noted that during 2002, that administration won its third successive victory at the polls.

National Youth Service

The National Youth Service (NYS) programme was established in the 1970s under the Manley regime as a means of providing on-the-job training for graduates from secondary schools, but it was dismantled during the Seaga-led government in one of its structural adjustment initiatives. In 1995, the Patterson administration formally reintroduced it, and in 1998, it established a legal framework to prevent it being dismantled in the future. Participants who had graduated from high school and were unable to enter college or university immediately were required to serve their country through work done at any government institution. The programme found favour with many young Jamaicans. The PNP campaign rhetoric during the 1989 elections had placed this issue on the political agenda of the country as a means of attracting young voters who had grown frustrated with the Seaga-led administration and were attracted to the prospect of the return of programmes such as the NYS.

Since its re-establishment, it has been training and providing on-the-job work experience for approximately two thousand youths each year. The organization is uniquely suited to effectively address many of the social issues facing young people in Jamaica. As a result, the NYS managed a number of programmes, including the following:

- The Corps Programme, a four-week career training and resocialization residential orientation, followed by six-month job placement, for high school graduates aged 17–24
- The Jamaica/Canada Youth Exchange, an annual youth exchange conducted in association with Canada World Youth focused on literacy projects
- The Jamaica Values and Attitudes Project for Tertiary Students (JAMVAT), providing partial payment of tuition fees in exchange for voluntary service
- The Information Communication Technology programme, a certificate course for people with disabilities
- The National Summer Employment Programme, which annually employs on average four thousand students islandwide during the summer holidays
- The NYS in Schools Project, geared towards instilling core values in high school students through service clubs
- The NYS Volunteerism Project, featuring periodic projects managed by the NYS in association with private sponsors; national, parish and community organizations; cadets; community members; and NYS participants

By 2006, approximately twelve thousand young people had benefited from the reintroduced NYS. As a result of the success of the NYS programme, the beneficiaries under the revamped NYS were major targets for the PNP during the elections of 1997 and 2002. All pre-eminent publications from the Patterson-led PNP during the elections included the reintroduced NYS.

Operation PRIDE

Operation PRIDE was developed to provide housing solutions to poor Jamaicans who were living on land owned by the state. It was a mechanism to regularize land tenure and to improve the housing conditions of these citizens. The acronym *PRIDE* means "Programme for Resettlement and Integrated Development Enterprise". The term *Operation* was added to *PRIDE* as a marketing mechanism, and it acknowledged that the Patterson administration was on a crusade to remedy the social strains and pressures of the previous two decades – the absence of an adequate settlement policy and the indiscriminate squatting and capturing of government and privately owned land.

In order to benefit, participants had to be a Jamaican over eighteen years old, not be the owner of a current home or lot, earn an annual income of less than US$14,285, and be able to show proof of ability to pay.

There were four main objectives of Operation PRIDE. The first was to meet the shelter needs of low-income Jamaicans through establishing new planned settlements, regularizing illegal settlements and upgrading existing ones. The second was improving environmental and public health conditions in settlements throughout the country. The third was mobilizing resources in the informal sector towards the improving and employing the people involved. The fourth was distributing government land as a catalyst in the whole process.

Those involved were required to become part of a provident scheme, where, for the construction of their houses and to build the infrastructure that was needed to make a decent community, they would match contributions made by government. Roads, sewage systems, water and light were all features of the infrastructure established, and over thirty thousand land titles and housing units were realized as a result of this initiative.

Operation PRIDE was regarded as an excellent programme by many individuals within the society. The initiative was, however, marred by allegations of corruption and fraud which had a deleterious effect on the Patterson-led administration and contributed to the reduction in public support for the PNP by the 2002 election.

Communication Strategies

It is clear that leaders and both political parties have sought to introduce social programmes and policies to improve the lives of citizens in modern Jamaica. The Manley regime of the 1970s was noted for introducing a compendium of social policies and programmes to improve the quality of life. Despite significant pressures brought to bear by multilateral institutions during the late 1970s and 1980s, the Manley and Seaga administrations sought to introduce programmes that would respond to the needs of citizens, as did the Patterson administration of the 1990s.

However, it was the communication strategies deployed in each instance that made the difference in the success levels of the programmes, and ultimately in the success of the leaders and the political parties. The Seaga administration introduced food stamps, HEART and ROSE programmes, and provided income tax exemption for people with disabilities. But in Seaga's bid for the elections of 1989, 1993, 1997 and 2002, he failed to remind and convince the electorate of the worth of these social programmes that he had implemented during the 1980s. For example, the ROSE programme was an excellent initiative to modernize the education system in Jamaica, but Seaga was unable to complete the reform because his government was voted out of office in the 1989 election. He failed to effectively communicate and ensure that there was awareness of this and other programmes and policies implemented, which could have encouraged citizen participation in the political process. The result was the election loss of his party, and the JLP was unable to win again until 2007.

Conversely, the PNP, under the leadership of Manley and Patterson, managed to win election after election as they constantly reminded citizens of the diverse social programmes that they introduced. It must be noted that while it was the Seaga administration that introduced programmes such as the food stamps and HEART, more citizens associated them with Patterson and the PNP because of the heavy and persistent communication focus on them. The PNP was able to convince the electorate that very little had been accomplished in the social sector by the Seaga-led JLP in the 1980s. These claims were supported by some social commentators in the media and members of the academic community. In *Consequences of Structural Adjustment,* Le Franc, Anderson and Witter chronicled the effects of the structural adjustment programme on the social sector in Jamaica during the 1980s (Le Franc 1994).

The social programmes described here, which were put in place by the Manley- and Patterson-led PNP, had a positive effect on a wide cross section of the population. They were launched and relaunched to great fanfare. The Patterson administration, for example, used all the available governmental and political party structures to promote these initiatives, and this yielded dividends for the PNP at the polls.

Once again, it is demonstrated that for a political administration to be successful, it has to have an effective communications strategy in place to market the product to citizens. Nationals will buy into the product if they have benefited from it, and they will support the political organization that has packaged and marketed its products effectively. The PNP regime between 1972 and 1976 did an excellent job at communicating its programmes and policies to citizens through Manley's talent at oratory and his connection with popular culture. The programmes and policies that were implemented were linked to the reggae recorded and distributed to citizens across the island. The Patterson administration of the 1990s also had a strategic approach to the marketing of varied social programmes implemented, and this contributed to four successive victories for the PNP up to 2002.

But by 2002, the signs were clear that the Seaga-led JLP was catching up to the PNP. The PNP won the 2002 elections by a margin of 34–26 seats. They had won the 1997 elections by a margin of 50–10. The JLP had picked up 16 more seats in 2002 than they had in 1997 – an approximately 160 per cent increase. The question now was: What contributed to this significant swing towards the JLP?

In this context, I believe the answer lies in a significant social policy initiative that was brought to the forefront of the campaign in 2002 that warrants a special examination. The Seaga-led JLP placed the issue of free education on the campaign agenda. It promised citizens that if elected, the JLP would introduce free education up to the secondary level. The issue resonated among voters because a significant portion of the population was experiencing difficulties in paying fees under the Patterson administration.

Free education was not a novel idea. In the 1970s, the Manley-led PNP had introduced free education up to the tertiary level. Because of this, the PNP had developed a reputation for supporting education but had not been able to deliver it consistently due to cost concerns. The reintroduction of the subject by the Seaga-led JLP triggered a passionate debate in the lead-up to the 2002 election.

Admittedly, the issue caught the PNP napping, and it was forced to develop a new approach towards the funding of education. For three years, it had had a cost-sharing mechanism in place. As an alternative, it now indicated that this would be phased out over a three-year period, starting in 2003 with a freezing of existing fees, and that free education would be introduced by 2005. The PNP also introduced the idea of paying for four Caribbean Examination Council exams – mathematics, English, computer science and a science subject – for all students at the high school level.

Introducing the issue of education in the campaign was extremely important. Both the PNP and the JLP were now utilizing the market as the model for managing the economy, and there were very few distinguishing features between the two political parties. The introduction of free education would have made a clear distinction between them. In a competitive political environment, the political party that is best able to present a difference in the eyes of the electorate is the one most likely to be victorious in an election. The narrowing of the gap between the PNP and the JLP in the 2002 election was now clear, with the issue of free education illustrating this point.

In the ongoing dialectic of political communication, the debate revolves around "freedom" and "order", prioritized by liberals and conservatives, respectively. The issue of education is a fundamental priority for those who support the "freedom" perspective. Powell, Bourne and Waller (2007) revealed that 53 per cent of the population were for "freedom", versus 43 per cent for "order". Although the conservative Seaga-led JLP was identified with order, having been out of power for a long time, it possibly recognized the need for a major shift in policy and opted for one that it felt would capture the imagination of Jamaican citizens.

Powell et al. (2007) also revealed that over 60 per cent of the respondents were not in favour of a market-driven economy, in which citizens are required to pay for goods and services. The Patterson-led PNP had liberalized the economy, and citizens were required to pay user fees and share costs for a number of social services, which included education. This sparked a great deal of ambivalence in the society.

There were three schools of thought on this matter. One was from the advocates of the free market system, who believed that citizens should pay for education based on the limited resources of the state and its inability to fully finance social services. Then there were those who believed that education should be free up to the secondary level, so people would still enjoy some degree of government subsidy, although they would be required to pay at the tertiary level. The third perspective was that it should be free at all levels, based on the view that education was the only means for correcting the grave social ills affecting Jamaican society. This view was also born out of the experience with the Manley administration of the 1970s, where the objective was for the average Jamaican to access all levels of the education system without any major encumbrance.

In Jamaica, free education is a policy that is often associated with democratic socialism and resonated with some citizens because of their experience with the Manley regime in the 1970s, and also because of the fact that more people favoured a middle-ground approach to economic management.

What the JLP proposed in the 2002 elections constituted a considerable policy shift. It was identifying education as the top socioeconomic priority, notwithstanding that it was under the Seaga regime of the 1980s that the payment of fees was introduced into the system. The organization was now embracing a policy initiative that it had opposed in the 1970s.

But while the idea of free education resonated among citizens, the Patterson-led PNP was able to secure victory. It was argued by some social commentators that this win was due to three main factors.

First, Seaga was not seen as a credible messenger promoting free education. The PNP marketed him as the man who had dismantled the education policies of Michael Manley in the 1980s, and as the man who first introduced fee payment for education. This helped to discredit the Seaga-led JLP, but not before it had made serious gains and increased its parliamentary seat count, mostly in constituencies with a strong middle class. Education was of fundamental importance to this group.

Second, there was some uncertainty among voters as to whether it was free education akin to that which had been introduced in the 1970s, or a modified policy initiative. This caused doubt in the minds of some voters.

Finally, the PNP was able to communicate and market a number of its socioeconomic achievements to the electorate in a convincing way through the publication of a document entitled *Solid Achievements* during the election campaign of 2002. The people were able to identify with the message of the PNP via this booklet, which highlighted tangible economic and social benefits such as PATH and HEART-NTA, with which they could identify.

One can conclude, therefore, that the effective communication of social programmes to citizens is a pre-eminent contributing factor to the success or failure of a leader and his or her administration. Voters are stimulated to participate in the political process when there is a good communication strategy and they anticipate that social programmes will have a direct beneficial impact on them. It must be noted that the Patterson-led PNP was more successful at the polls than the Manley-led PNP and the Seaga-led JLP because it had a more effective communication strategy for social programmes.

Whether it is through the structures of the PNP, the Live and Direct initiative by Patterson or the Face-to-Face initiative by ministers and members of Parliament, the Patterson-led PNP was most effective at marketing its social programmes. The responsiveness of citizens to these communication strategies were manifested in and evidenced by the outcomes of the multiple elections won by the Patterson-led PNP.

6.

Communicating Programmes and Policies Relating to the Regional and International Agendas

In any modern democratic society, international and regional affairs are of paramount importance. This is because since the early 1990s, the world has effectively collapsed into a global village. However, since the 1950s, the stage had been set for the development of an interdependent world through the establishment of the IMF and the General Agreement on Tariffs and Trade (GATT). The GATT has since evolved into the WTO and is the principal agency which sets the rules and parameters for trade across the globe.

Since the collapse of communism in the early 1990s, the world has been dominated by policies revolving around a market philosophy. This is because of the hegemonic role that the United States has been required to play, coupled with the presence of the IMF and the WTO. Jamaica has been obliged to participate in this ongoing transformation.

Since attaining independence in 1962, Jamaica has made its presence felt on the global stage. It has emphatically made its voice heard on issues such as apartheid, a system of racial segregation that existed in South Africa, and it has consistently advocated for more resources to be made available to developing countries by richer nations, especially those which had exploited the resources of the poorer nations through colonization.

Since 1962, both the JLP and the PNP have sought to carve out their foreign policy niches. The JLP's conservative approach was aptly captured in a statement made by its founder, Bustamante, who, when asked what was his party's foreign policy, replied, "We are with the West." This clearly indicated that to preserve the country's image, the JLP was prepared to support whatever stance the major Western states took on international issues.

Regionally, the JLP, while embracing the Caribbean Community (CARICOM), consistently placed its emphasis on relating to countries to the north. To focus on CARICOM, it believed, was to limit and restrict the potential of Jamaica where international trade was concerned. This is why efforts were made by the JLP to abandon Jamaica's quest to intensify its participation in the West India Federation in the early 1960s. In the referendum of 1961, the JLP clearly campaigned against this regional initiative and caused the leader of Trinidad and Tobago, one of Jamaica's regional partners, Eric Williams, to make that famous statement, "One from 10 leaves zero."

Conversely, the PNP adopted a more liberal approach towards foreign policy, guided by its party's constitution, which embraces a democratic socialist philosophy. Its regional and international positions are guided by the following objectives (PNP 2008, 2):

> To cooperate with labour and socialist organisations within the Commonwealth with a view to promoting the purposes of the Party and, more particularly, to take common action with such organisations in the Caribbean region for the promotion of a higher standard of social and economic life for the population of the respective countries of the region as a whole;
>
> To cooperate with labour and socialist organisations in other countries for the improvement of the social and economic standards and conditions of the peoples of the world.

Therefore, administrations formed by the PNP since gaining political independence have tended to be more radical in their approach to foreign policy, and very outspoken in the international arena. Regionally, PNP-led administrations have always embraced CARICOM, seeing it as a means of uniting the Caribbean to face the challenges of a progressively globalized world. PNP administrations have supported CARICOM and prioritized a number of issues, such as the move to establish a regional single market and economy.

Apartheid in South Africa

Upon assuming the office of prime minister in 1972, Michael Manley articulated his administration's position on a number of international and regional issues. One of these statements was to denounce the system of government in South Africa – apartheid – which was established to deliberately discriminate and dehumanize the black majority. Past Jamaican leaders, such as Bustamante, Marcus Garvey and Norman Manley, had voiced their views on the subject in various international forums. As a matter of fact, Norman Manley joined forces with the Indian government to lead a boycott against South African–produced goods in the 1950s. This was the first international boycott against the apartheid South African regime.

Michael Manley believed that the system of apartheid was an injustice to humanity, and therefore, he spent a great deal of time opposing it in multiple international forums, such as the United Nations. The UN General

Assembly is an international body that includes both developed and developing countries and provides an opportunity through which states can express their views on a variety of issues affecting the individual states or other state parties. Speaking to the General Assembly in 1978, Manley (1978, 2) declared:

> If our research reveals that the League of Nations was petitioned 50 years ago – long before the word "apartheid" entered the political vocabulary – how does it happen that we are today seeking to mobilize world opinion afresh in 1978? How does a world that produced Lincoln, Marx, Lenin, Mao and Franklin Roosevelt still stand impotent before the vicious edifice of shame and degradation? Apartheid has been denounced by every significant political leader of the 20th century. It has been the subject of political indignation. It has been officially declared a crime against humanity. How, then, does this great Assembly of nations stand mocked by South Africa's unyielding position with respect to its racial policies? What of the latest rejection of the will of the United Nations in Namibia?

The discourse on the system of apartheid was articulated by Manley in every conceivable international forum. In 1978, he was among a group of prominent leaders awarded a gold medal from the United Nations for their outstanding contribution to the struggle against apartheid.

The opposition of the Manley regime towards apartheid in South Africa reflected local sentiments on this system of government. Jamaicans were outraged that the regime in South Africa had incarcerated leaders of the African National Congress, such as Nelson Mandela. The rage against this indignity was expressed in reggae by popular artists such as Bob Marley, Jimmy Cliff and Peter Tosh. The efforts of Manley and other leaders contributed to the release of Mandela from prison, and to the dismantling of the apartheid system in the early 1990s.

The New International Economic Order

Michael Manley also advocated for the establishment of the New International Economic Order (NIEO). As early as the mid-1960s, there were discussions in the United Nations to have greater cooperation between the north and the south, which led to the establishment of the Group of 77 (G77) countries. This came within the context of growing economic challenges among developing countries, and it was felt among the G77 that greater dialogue was needed with the developed countries to resolve some of these issues. The efforts of the G77 gained momentum in the 1970s with the arrival on the world stage of leaders such as Manley. He established himself as a strong advocate for developing countries and effectively employed his ability to articulate issues and champion the cause of the G77 members.

One area in which he made a significant impact was in the campaign for the establishment of an NIEO. Developed countries were paying very cheap prices for the products of developing countries, which they would then refine and resell on the open market at exorbitant prices. This created a global economic imbalance and resulted in glaring disparities in the standard of living between countries of the north and south.

Manley and other world leaders used various international forums to push for a change in this system, contributing to the forging of what is regarded as South-South Cooperation. Through this mechanism, developing countries would forge stronger links with each other in the trading of goods and services in order to effect better pricing mechanisms and ultimately reduce the economic imbalance between north and south.

Locally, Manley used every conceivable avenue to articulate this particular international policy. Whether it was in Parliament, on national television and radio broadcasts or at annual conferences of the PNP, the matter was placed before Jamaican citizens.

Similar to the efforts to establish the NIEO was that for the creation of the New Information and Communication Order (NWICO). The NWICO is a political proposal emerging from discussions among countries within the Non-Aligned Movement (NAM). The discussion and proposal were developed in the late 1970s and continued throughout the 1980s. The proposal was formulated within the United Nations Education, Science and Cultural Organization through the leadership of Irish diplomat Sean McBride. The proposal was included in a report titled *Many Voices, One World: Towards a New, More Just and More Efficient World Information and Communication Order* (International Commission for the Study of Communication Problems 1980). It was a serious attempt by countries within the Global South to democratize the international communication system (Padovani 2008).

Manley was an extremely powerful voice among NAM leaders, and it was inconceivable for him not to be involved in this debate. It was the view of both him and his colleagues that the Global North had dominated the information and communication system, controlling the production of technology, ownership of media, distribution of information and determination of content. The global information and communication agenda was being determined primarily by players in the Global North and countries within the Global South were seen as mere consumers. This never found favour with the leaders of the NAM, and they were very emphatic in their quest to democratize the international information and communication system.

Manley's efforts to push for NIEO and NWICO saw limited success during his lifetime. However, it must be noted that the current shift in the global economic order can in part be attributed to his work towards the creation of NIEO and NWICO. Countries such as China, India, Brazil and South Africa were all members of the NAM and emerged as modern economic giants. Through these countries, the vision of the NIEO and the NWICO is being realized. The United Nations Development Programme (UNDP) global development report projected that by 2020, for the first time, production of goods and services in Brazil, India, China and South Africa would surpass that of all the developed countries in the north combined (UNDP 2013). Similarly, the world has seen the advent of Al Jazeera, a global media giant emanating from Qatar, one of the countries in the Global South. It has been providing news and other serious content to citizens throughout the world since 1996.

Regional Integration

As pointed out earlier in this chapter, the PNP always had a positive attitude towards CARICOM and placed significant emphasis on this regional institution. Indeed, the Manley regime brought Jamaica into CARICOM and was one of its first signatories in 1974 (CARICOM 2011). Regional integration was a core principle of the foreign policy of both Manley and his party, which articulated the principle of embracing regional institutions in its constitution (PNP 2008). They believed that a unified Caribbean would be able to successfully tackle some of the economic challenges confronting developing countries, and Manley used the parliamentary budget debates in Jamaica as the major mechanism of articulating policy issues on CARICOM. In turn, Delano Franklyn (2009) confirms that he was hailed by CARICOM as the quintessential Caribbean man. Whether it was on issues relating to trade, cricket, politics, Cuba or any other matter that would enhance regional development, Manley was a strong advocate.

Anticommunist Posture

In 1980, Seaga became prime minister for the first time. During the election campaign, he positioned himself as being strongly anticommunist. He formed alliances with the Republican Party in the United States and strongly denounced communism in every available forum. He also presented himself as an advocate for the free market system, which he believed went hand in hand with an anticommunist posture. This also formed a foundational part of Seaga and the JLP's message that they were better managers of the economy, as they emphasized fiscal prudence and allowing the private sector to be the engine of growth in the economy.

The Manley-led PNP administration had established close diplomatic relationships with communist states such as Cuba and the USSR, and this presented a perfect backdrop against which Seaga pitched his anticommunist campaign. In 1979, when the Manley government terminated its borrowing relationship with the IMF, Seaga viewed it as a hostile act against the United States and the major institutions of capitalism in the world. Jamaica was experiencing hard economic times, and Seaga linked this difficult environment to the ending of the IMF connection. On the basis of that belief, the Seaga-led JLP transformed the meaning of the letters IMF to "It's Manley's Fault". In any political campaign, such a meaning has to be construed as an excellent communication strategy geared at blaming the opponent for the demise of the economic fortunes of the country. Seaga was conscious of the prevailing arguments in the public sphere as it related to communism and cleverly sought to exploit the discussion to his political advantage. This is what Habermas (1989) alluded to in referring to discussion in the public sphere as a critical part of the policy-formulation mechanism.

After a gruelling campaign and a bitterly contested election in 1980, in which over eight hundred citizens died due to political violence, the JLP emerged victorious in a landslide, holding fifty-one of the sixty seats across the island. It is clear that Seaga's posturing as a strong anticommunist and a procapitalist advocate assisted in the political fortunes of his party. Seaga was projected as "the deliverer". Citizens had grown frustrated with the Manley administration; they blamed him and the PNP for the economic catastrophe of the country. Moreover, they believed that the international posture of Manley as a strong supporter for the Castro regime in Cuba was too confrontational towards the United States. As a result, Seaga's promotion of an anticommunist posture was timely and appropriate in the eyes of the Jamaican people.

Here, we can see that the victory of Seaga at the polls was largely attributable to the fact that there was an effective communication strategy in place. This was the case because Seaga enjoyed the confidence of the capitalist class at the time, and so access to funding for his campaign was not a major problem. He was thus able to use an array of communication channels to articulate his policy positions on national issues – television, radio, print media and community meetings were all used, as well as speeches in Parliament.

Grenada

As prime minister of Jamaica, Seaga continued his anticommunist posture and procapitalist advocacy. These were to play a considerable role as a serious international situation unfolded in Grenada. In 1979, Maurice Bishop and his New Jewel Movement overthrew the Eric Gairy regime and seized the reins of power in that country. Bishop disbanded all political parties and established close connections with communist states such as Cuba and the USSR. But some of his fellow ministers, such as Bernard Coard, the deputy prime minister, felt that he was not moving fast enough to establish scientific socialism.

In October 1983, Bishop and his administration were overthrown by his own colleagues and assassinated in a bloody coup. This violent act threw that country into chaos, and the Organisation of Eastern Caribbean States and its governor general, Sir Paul Scoon, requested help from the United States to repel the coup and re-establish democracy in the island. According to Seaga (2009), countries within the region felt that the insurgents would attempt to create another communist regime in the Caribbean and that this would have serious consequences for the US-Caribbean relationship.

The US administration, led by President Reagan, would not countenance this situation. The US had just experienced a hostage crisis in Beirut, where a number of Americans had been killed. Over one thousand Americans were living in Grenada at the time, and Reagan was only too anxious to stamp his hegemonic authority on the region.

By this time, Seaga had established himself as the major supportive voice for the United States in the Caribbean. He was strident in his criticism of communism and openly embraced US foreign policy. He saw Bishop's overthrow as a moment to reconsolidate his position as "America's man" in the Caribbean. He condemned the action in Grenada and immediately began mobilizing forces to repel the coup. The establishment of another communist state on the doorstep of the United States would be an affront to the Monroe Doctrine. This dominant principle of US policy, originated by President James Monroe in 1823, stated that any intervention by external powers in the politics of the Americas is a hostile act against the United States. The Reagan administration launched an invading force in which US troops were supported by contingents from the Caribbean, including Jamaica and Puerto Rico. Just over eight thousand troops participated in the invasion, dubbed "Operation Urgent Fury".

The Order Paper of Jamaica's Parliament provided for any member of either the Senate or the House of Representatives to put forth for debate in Parliament motions of public interest. In October 1983, Deputy Prime Minister Shearer tabled a resolution seeking approval from the highest decision-making body to support the government's efforts to assist in restoring democracy in Grenada. A full debate on the matter was facilitated by the JLP-led government, by the end of which Seaga had secured parliamentary support for the operation.

Once again, he scored big points in the public's eyes on a significant regional and foreign policy initiative. He was seen by Jamaican citizens as a tough leader who was decisive and had major political connections which made things happen. Moreover, the anticommunist political propaganda of the 1980 election left doubts in the minds of Jamaicans as to the effectiveness of communism as a system of government. Therefore, for this system to be established in a "sister" Caribbean island would be construed as a retrograde step. Seaga's political capital soared; public opinion polls showed his approval rating at over 50 per cent for the first time since the 1980 election.

The political landscape that emerged in Jamaica after the Grenada invasion was what political strategists regarded as a perfect opportunity for a leader under the Westminster system to take the initiative. Seaga did not allow it to pass because he understood clearly that hard economic decisions had to be taken and the moment had to be exploited. The promise of economic deliverance and the transformation of the economy had proved elusive in the previous three years, so he had to seize the moment in order to continue as prime minister.

Seaga called a snap election without any hesitation. The PNP, led by Michael Manley, failed to even contest the election held on 15 December 1983, arguing that Seaga had broken a commitment not to call any elections until there were reforms to the electoral voting system. The JLP took control of all sixty seats in Parliament, and Seaga became prime minister for the second time. For the first time in Jamaica's political history, Parliament was completely controlled by one political party.

The Caribbean Court of Justice

The PNP administration led by Prime Minister Patterson in the 1990s adopted several radical approaches with regard to its regional and international policies. After approximately fifty years of deliberation over the issue in the region, in 2002, the Patterson administration took the decision to establish the Caribbean Court of Justice (CCJ) as the final appellate court of Jamaica. This was within the context of years of subscription to the Privy Council in the United Kingdom as the final appellate body in the justice system of Jamaica. Public sentiments were that the Privy Council had served Jamaica well in general, but it was time for the final court of the country to be brought closer to home. It had been posited that its distance was too expensive for individuals to access, and ordinary people should be able to use the final appellate body more easily.

In 2000, the leaders of CARICOM resolved that after having the discussion about the final appellate court for the past fifty years, it was time for action.

Consequently, a path to establish the CCJ as the final appeal court for countries within CARICOM was outlined. The challenge was in establishing respect for it as the binding authority of its decisions, while ensuring public support and confidence in its administration of justice.

As an appeal court, the CCJ was designed to give moral leadership to Caribbean societies. As an international court, it would ensure that the regional international movement developed along a structured, sustainable and rule-based manner. More important, as the tribunal responsible for interpreting and applying the Revised Treaty of Chaguaramas, which established CARICOM, including the CARICOM Single Market and Economy (CSME), the CCJ was to be the guarantor of the rights accorded to nationals. Important in this context were the rights of skilled professionals to practise their professions in any jurisdiction of CARICOM, and for artisans and workers with other specified categories of skills to provide services as independent contractors in any area of CARICOM.

The court was to function in two jurisdictions – an original jurisdiction and an appellate jurisdiction. In its appellate jurisdiction, the CCJ would apply the laws of the member-states from which it was hearing appeals. In the exercise of its original jurisdiction, the CCJ would perform the role of an international court, applying rules of international law in interpreting and applying the revised Treaty of Chaguaramas.

In terms of staffing, the Regional Judicial and Legal Services Commission was established and given responsibility for the appointment of judges and other court employees. The court comprised a president who was chairman of the commission and at least nine judges who would also determine wages, salaries and conditions of work.

A trust fund was set up to finance the court and was intended to insulate it from political interference. The fund was managed by a board of trustees. The agreement establishing the fund was signed by members that attended the Twenty-Fourth Heads of Government Conference held in Montego Bay, Jamaica. The seat of the court is in Trinidad and Tobago, but as circumstances warrant, it may sit in the territory of any other contracting party.

The JLP was opposed to the establishment of the CCJ, despite the fact that it had approved the move to establish such a court in 1988 at a meeting of CARICOM heads. However, they argued that it was not timely for Jamaica to leave the Privy Council; instead, it proposed that Jamaica should subscribe to the CCJ only in its original jurisdiction and after a period of time, based on the experience, it could become a member of the court in its final appellate form.

The Patterson administration objected to this position. However, in order to establish the CCJ as the final appellate court, it was necessary to amend the

Jamaica Constitution, which required either securing a two-thirds majority in both houses of Parliament or having a referendum approved by the public.

Public sentiment on the matter was divided as it became increasingly politically controversial. Members of civil society took an active interest in the debate and decided to challenge the government in court. The matter was heard in the Constitutional Court, and the judges ruled in favour of the government. The matter was further taken to the Appeal Court by members of civil society, and again the Court ruled in favour of the government. However, members of civil society were steadfast in their determination to ensure that their views were heard at all levels of the judicial process, and they brought the matter to the Privy Council. All of these actions by civil society were supported by the JLP.

The judges at the Privy Council ruled in favour of the members of civil society, led by the Independent Council of Jamaica on Human Rights, and stated that in order for the government to abolish appeals to the Privy Council and establish another final appellate body, it had to be entrenched in the constitution. According to the judges at the Privy Council (2004, 14): "The Board is driven to conclude that the three Acts, taken together, do have the effect of undermining the protection given to the people of Jamaica by entrenched provisions of Chapter VII of the Constitution. From this it follows that the procedure appropriate for amendment of an entrenched provision should have been followed."

This constituted a major setback for the administration. Patterson thought that it would not be politically possible to get the necessary support in either Parliament or a referendum, and further, that it was politically prudent for both the opposition and government to agree on the matter. But no amount of negotiation could convince the JLP to relax its position on such a fundamental constitutional decision.

The Patterson administration was then forced to relax its stance on a pre-eminent regional and national issue. It chose to establish a mechanism that would allow the country to submit appeals to the CCJ in its original jurisdiction – that is, on matters relating to issues coming out of the multiple agreements that were entered into through CARICOM. This was eventually supported by the JLP.

In all of this, one has to examine the communication strategy of the Patterson administration with regard to the CCJ, which revealed serious shortcomings. While there were ministerial statements and ministry papers tabled in Parliament and numerous press releases and discussions in the media, there were no Live and Direct and very limited Face-to-Face sessions by Patterson in the respective constituencies, the dominant communication vehicles which had been used in the mid-1990s. It must be noted that some members of the

Patterson administration were not very passionate about the matter, which resulted in very few cabinet members venturing out to promote the CCJ to the public. The lack of marketing this major, far-reaching national policy contributed to the thwarting of the Patterson-led administration in its bid to establishing the CCJ as a final appellate court of Jamaica. Once again, the JLP managed to outmanoeuvre the PNP on another foreign affairs issue.

CARICOM Single Market and Economy

Since the early 1990s, changing global realities have been forcing countries and states to formulate new approaches to capitalize on the opportunities of a globalized world. The Caribbean was no exception to this. Consequently, the leaders of CARICOM took the decision to establish the CSME in order to ensure that the Caribbean was able to better respond to the challenges of globalization. As far back as 1989, at the annual CARICOM Heads of Government Conference held at Grand Anse, Grenada, leaders took certain strategic decisions meant to herald the Caribbean into the twenty-first century. These included:

- Deepening economic integration by advancing beyond a common market, towards a single market and economy
- Widening the membership and thereby expanding the economic mass of CARICOM – thus, Suriname and Haiti were admitted as full members in 1995 and 2002, respectively
- Progressive insertion of the region into the global trading and economic system by strengthening trading links with nontraditional partners

This was achieved through a series of bilateral trade agreements with Venezuela, Colombia, the Dominican Republic, Cuba and, more recently, Costa Rica, as well as by full and effective participation in multilateral and other major trade negotiations, such as the WTO, the renegotiation of the Lomé and Cotonou arrangements with the European Union and the Free Trade Area of the Americas.

The Patterson administration was instrumental in ensuring that Jamaica played a leading role in establishing the CSME, because the country was vital to developing the framework for its establishment at the Revised Treaty of Chaguaramas. According to Kenneth Hall, the primary objective was to create a seamless economic space in which goods, services, people and capital could move freely throughout the region (Hall and Chuck-A-Sang 2007).

The efforts to establish a regional trading block had two components. The first was the establishment of the Caribbean Single Market (CSM). This mechanism sought to promote the free movement of goods and services, as well as skills and Caribbean nationals. This segment was launched in January 2006, and three countries (Jamaica, Barbados, and Trinidad and Tobago) signed the document and brought it into effect.

The second phase of this development in the Caribbean was the establishment of the CSME in 2008. During this phase, it was proposed to implement the harmonization of economic policies such as a single currency and other unified economic policies.

The Patterson administration was adamant about the introduction of the CSM and CSME. It had tabled varied ministry papers in Parliament and passed legislation such as the Caribbean Community Act of 2004 to facilitate the implementation of these important regional initiatives. However, notwithstanding their importance, concerns remained about what they would bring to Jamaica, as well as the level of knowledge that existed among the Jamaican people about them (Bourne and Attzs 2005). According to Seaga, the CSME would not bring much to Jamaica. While he supported the move to strengthen the relationship with other Caribbean territories, he claimed that Jamaica's future lay in deepening and consolidating the relationship with neighbours to the north: "They have a larger market and they have greater disposable income that would be beneficial to Jamaica" (Jamaica Hansard 2002).

Patterson held a different view, stating the following: "Global realities dictate that in order for one to maximize the benefits of the globalized world, countries have to move together. This is why countries are enjoining themselves into trading and economic blocks" (Jamaica Hansard 2002).

But while the leaders of the distinct political organizations had an understanding as to the advantages and disadvantages of the CSM and CSME, citizens were yet to do so. There had not been a comprehensive communication strategy to market this important regional initiative to the people. It must be noted that while the Face-to-Face programme was adopted to facilitate dialogue with the people on the issue, Live and Direct was not, and its absence from the political dialogue with citizens dampened the enthusiasm of Jamaicans towards the CSME. The prime minister, as the ultimate leader and facilitator of the Live and Direct programme, was absent, and citizens generally take their cue from their leaders. In order to give credibility and believability to any major public policy or programme, the presence of the prime minister was absolutely necessary.

The Iraq War

In March 2003, the United States invaded Iraq. This act fell within the context of the "war on terror" after the attack by al-Qaeda on the World Trade Centre, the

Pentagon, and other locations within the country on 11 September 2001, and the US accusation that Iraqi leader Saddam Hussein was producing weapons of mass destruction. Members of the United Nations had voted in several resolutions for Iraq to allow UN weapons inspectors to verify whether that country was in possession of these weapons. Saddam Hussein refused to comply, and an international conflict emerged with the United States. The US president, George W. Bush, asked Congress in March 2003 to declare war on Iraq because it was the belief of his administration that it posed a threat to the United States and the world. The regime in Iraq was also accused of harbouring and funding terrorists, as the Bush administration believed that Saddam's government was supporting the al-Qaeda group.

In a resolution designed to place pressure on Saddam's administration and to force them to comply with UN weapons inspectors, members of the Security Council overwhelmingly voted to adopt resolution 1441 in November 2002, which required Iraq to comply with the United Nations and to have its weapon inspectors conduct an independent audit for weapons of mass destruction.

By December 2002, Iraq provided the United Nations with a document containing over twelve thousand pages on its weapons programme. However, this did not satisfy most members of the UN Security Council because they did not believe the contents of the report. As a result, some members were determined to get the weapons inspectors to conduct a search. Active diplomacy was taking place up to March 2003, but by this time, President Bush had made up his mind to send troops into Iraq to topple the Saddam regime.

Several members of the United Nations were very much opposed to this approach. They felt that the Bush administration had violated the UN's bylaws and that the UN weapons inspectors should be given more time to complete their work. Jamaica was one such country that voiced its concerns, and these were made known in the corridors of the United Nations.

The invasion was of intrinsic importance to Jamaica, as it had direct implications for the economy. Each year, it spends approximately 60 per cent of its import bill on oil. Any movement on the international market for the price of oil was bound to have a deleterious effect on the Jamaican economy. Iraq had five times the oil reserves as the United States and was a vital player in determining its price. Jamaica's stance on the invasion had causal implications in its pricing model. This is why it was important for the government to update citizens as to the consequences of the war in Iraq and the basis for its opposition.

Jamaica held the view that the weapons inspectors should be allowed to complete their task. According to a *Jamaica Observer* article ("Damage Control", 21 March 2003), Jamaica's opposition to the US decision to invade Iraq at the United Nations caused some tension between Washington and Kingston. This followed a statement first uttered by President Bush in 2001, "You're either with us or against us in the fight against terror" (CNN 2001). It clearly placed those who opposed the US path or abstained on a principled and independent basis in an anti-US group and put a strain on US diplomatic relations with various states, including Jamaica.

While the government of Jamaica took the decision not to support the US invasion of Iraq, very little was said to the people about the real issues. It was left to the media to disseminate information to citizens. Again, there were no Live and Direct or Face-to-Face sessions to communicate what was taking place. The absence of clear directives from the Patterson administration on the matter resulted in public whispers and disquiet.

Thus far, this discussion points to the Patterson-led PNP administration having more success at communicating its programmes and policies and winning elections than the Manley- and Seaga-led administrations. However, the examples given in this chapter highlight times when the administration fell short when it came to effectively communicating regional and international policies to the people. The three cases involving the Patterson-led PNP administration described here all show deficiencies in the administration's handling of the communication and marketing of regional and international policies. This resulted in the Patterson regime giving way to political pressure from the Jamaican public, as in the case of the CCJ, which no doubt contributed to the results of the election in 2002 which, although the PNP won, it was with a smaller majority than the previous election. The majority of only thirty-four to twenty-six constituted one of the closest margins for a national election since Jamaica gained political independence in 1962.

From the data presented in this chapter, one can draw some conclusions regarding the knowledge of citizens relating to international and regional policies:

- The extent of the knowledge, it seems, is heavily dependent on the degree to which the policy would give either of the leaders and the political parties a competitive advantage. The leader and the political party will consistently highlight a foreign or regional policy matter that it deems to be advantageous. It will form part of its communication strategy if there is a significant possibility of soliciting a favourable election outcome. This is what Jamaica experienced over the period described here.
- The deliberate nature of a leader and his political organization to communicate foreign policies to citizens is heavily dependent on the political advantage that they are likely to derive from communicating such policies. Foreign policies can be very technical in nature. There

must, therefore, be a concentrated effort for political leaders and their political parties to disaggregate the policies in understandable proportions for citizens. The JLP has managed to do this over the years. Its founder, Alexander Bustamante, declared from the 1960s that "we are with the West", which has guided the foreign policy directions of the JLP over the years and has contributed to the political fortunes of that organization. Conversely, the PNP, while its leaders have adopted some radical and transformative foreign policies, has not been able to "jamalize" and effectively communicate these policies. Therefore, the party has not benefited politically. The cases highlighted in this chapter have shown the PNP being outmanoeuvred by the JLP on issues of foreign policy several times over the years. The organization and its leaders have not been breaking down foreign policies so they can communicate to citizens effectively.

- The JLP has been more successful in communicating foreign policy approaches and has yielded greater political benefits than the PNP. The cases described in this chapter demonstrate that the Seaga administration has had a greater electoral advantage from its regional and foreign policy approaches. This was demonstrated in the context of the Grenada invasion and the rhetoric adopted by the Seaga regime towards communism. In both instances, the Seaga-led administration enjoyed political success as well as economic gain. The United States injected significant cash into the Jamaican economy through different donor agencies, and in the context of the Grenada invasion, the JLP, under the leadership of Seaga, emerged victorious in the 1983 snap election.

This was not the first time that Jamaica saw the JLP outmanoeuvring the PNP on a vital foreign affairs issue and gaining political success. In the referendum of 1961, for instance, the JLP opted not to support joining the West Indies Federation because it believed that doing so would weaken Jamaica's quest to become a fully independent nation. The PNP, which was profederation, was defeated on this matter. As a consequence, the premier, Norman Manley, called a general election in 1962, in which the PNP was also defeated.

7.

Political Campaigning in Jamaica

To appreciate the intricacies of the communication strategies employed in political campaigning in Jamaica, particularly between 1972 and 2006, it is useful to be reminded of some of the theories upon which I draw in my analysis. Those most relevant to this discussion are briefly described here:

- Habermas (1989) defined the public sphere as a virtual or imaginary community which does not necessarily exist in any identifiable space. In its ideal form, the public sphere is "made up of private people gathered together as a public and articulating the needs of society with the state".
- Hall et al. (1973) state that media texts are encoded by the producer, meaning that whoever produces the text fills it with values and messages. The text is then decoded by the audience.
- Lasswell's (1948) model of communication describes an act of communication by defining who said it, what was said, in what channel it was said, to whom it was said, and with what effect it was said.
- McLuhan (1964) coined the phrase "The medium is the message", meaning that the nature of a medium (the channel through which a message is transmitted) is more important than the actual meaning or content of the message.

The 1972 election constituted an interesting period for political campaigning in Jamaica. However, before I venture into a qualitative description of elections and campaigns in the 1970s, 1980s and 1990s, it is prudent to review the types of leaders that have led Jamaica and the nature of their relationship with the Jamaican people.

Undoubtedly the personality of a leader is important to the success or failure of an administration. Global indicators have pointed to a number of political leaders that have played a dominant role in the success of their administrations, such as British prime minister Winston Churchill and, more recently, US president Bill Clinton. In their leadership roles, both built relationships with their public, as this is extremely important for political mobilization and participation. Here in Jamaica, the trajectory has been no different.

The foundational argument being posited in this book is that the success or failure of a leader and his or her political organization is closely linked to the effectiveness of their strategy for communicating their programmes and policies to their constituents. Therefore, the ability of a leader to connect and communicate with the masses is quintessential. Indeed, following Lasswell's (1948) basic Theory of Communication, it is imperative to know and understand the leading actors who are communicating with the people through the vehicle of the political parties. Moreover, it is important to understand that in the context of political communication, the messages of political parties are by and large leader-centric. In both the presidential model and the Westminster system, the leader drives the message, so it is prudent for us to understand the types of leadership personalities that have been involved with the body politic of Jamaica.

Edward Seaga was an anthropologist by training and had a vivid understanding of Jamaica's folk culture. He had done extensive study of reggae, Pocomania and Kumina, which are major art forms/religions of the country. Seaga was also involved in the production of reggae in the early 1960s and later sold his production company to Byron Lee, who went on to become an iconic figure in Jamaica's music scene. Seaga's involvement with the culture allowed him to build close relationships with Jamaican nationals, which later would play an indispensable role in his political career.

Seaga's ascendancy to the helm of the JLP injected new energy into that political organization and Jamaica as a whole. Stone (1992) described him as a technocratic leader with autocratic tendencies. Seaga, however, had a witty disposition and could use short, catchy phrases to communicate with his audience. He was the first non–trade union leader to lead the JLP, and he served two terms as prime minister.

Conversely, in the PNP, the departure of Norman Manley saw the entrance of another charismatic leader, his son Michael Manley. The younger Manley was a broadcaster by profession and had extensive experience in trade unionism. This combination was to be a significant asset for him, as his trade union work allowed him to build a solid relationship with the Jamaican people and, as Franklyn (2009) points out, he was able to charm the Jamaican people through his public addresses and negotiating skills. Described as eloquent and charismatic, he led the PNP until 1992, when P.J. Patterson assumed leadership of the party.

Patterson was a lawyer by profession. He was also a qualified teacher, having attended Bethlehem Teachers College and taught at Cornwall College for three years. He was often regarded as a technocratic leader with a laissez-faire approach to leadership (Munroe 2002). He too was involved in Jamaica's culture in the early 1960s through one of the country's major musical bands, the Skatalites. His musical involvement, coupled with his legal career, helped him to build a positive relationship with a broad cross section of the Jamaican population. He became the first non–trade unionist to have led the PNP.

It is quite evident that until the 1989 elections, Jamaican politics was dominated by charismatic leaders who had personalities that were appealing to the masses, which enabled them to communicate effectively with the public. These leaders also had a very good understanding of the national culture, and as such, they were able to identify with citizens in diverse ways. They immersed themselves into the culture of the society or became leaders in the major trade unions. The dominance of trade unions had been a signal characteristic of Jamaican politics up until 1989. However, all of this was transformed on the assumption of leadership in the political parties by Seaga and Patterson.

Over the years, leaders of political parties found creative ways to identify with citizens. This is where the "who" in Lasswell's theory applies. The communication process becomes easier when citizens (that is, the audience) can identify with their leaders. It makes any message more credible and believable.

Accordingly, the argument is presented by this author that *the success or failure of a political administration hinges on an effective communication strategy*. It must be understood that in the context of a democratic society, the ultimate test to determine the success or failure of an administration is an election. It is through elections that citizens express their views on the stewardship of a political administration. This is where the ordinary person gets an opportunity to express dissatisfaction or satisfaction with the programmes and policies that are being implemented by leaders and their administrations. This is where Lasswell's "what" and the effects of his theory become obvious.

It is, therefore, prudent to do a qualitative description of the issues which featured prominently in the elections between 1972 and 2006, and to determine whether they contributed to successful outcomes for the leaders and their political parties. By doing this, the objective of determining which leader has been most successful in communicating programmes and policies to citizens of Jamaica can be realized. Consequently, I thoroughly examine the elections of 1972, 1976, 1980, 1983, 1989, 1993, 1997 and 2002 in this chapter, and also look at the communication strategies used to articulate the issues to the public, particularly the themes used by the leaders and political parties.

The 1972 Election

The year 1972 constituted a critical juncture in Jamaica's history. It was about ten years after the country had gained political independence and therefore constituted a point at which one could truly assess the progress of the nation after colonization. It was the first time that the country was seeing elections contested without the dominant political parties being led by their founders, Norman Manley and Alexander Bustamante.

Hugh Lawson Shearer was the prime minister and leader of the JLP. He had taken the reins of power from Donald Sangster, who died shortly after taking office as prime minister in 1967. Shearer was a renowned trade unionist and had an established working relationship with the working class. He assumed leadership of the country at a time when the economy was growing at a fast pace – between 5 and 6 per cent. But while the economy was growing, there was a scarcity of jobs and inequity in the society was increasing. Social tension was high and contributed to riots in the country. Of note were riots in 1968 which were precipitated by the government's declaration of Walter Rodney, the University of the West Indies's black Guyanese lecturer and scholar, as persona non grata. Social tensions spilled over into the 1970s and formed the background for the 1972 election.

But there were changes in the leadership of the PNP as well. In 1969, Norman Manley retired, which paved the way for a new leader. His son, Michael, who had great knowledge of and respect for the workers, emerged as his successor. The stage was now set for an epic election battle between Manley and Shearer, two charismatic leaders with strong trade union connections, in the 1972 elections.

Due to the social tensions in the Jamaican society, the dialogue in the public sphere was being driven by the issues affecting citizens, such as education, health care, social and class inequality and unemployment.

It is noteworthy that by 1972, popular culture in the form of local reggae had become a dominant part of public discourse. Groups such as Bob Marley and the Wailers were gaining popularity, at least in part because they articulated the challenges of citizens in their music. Songs such as "Better Must Come" and "Dem Afi Get a Beaten" were all reflecting the mood and discontent among citizens in the country. Michael Manley immersed himself in this popular culture and used his political platform to speak about social ills. The popular music of the time became an integral part of the campaign strategy of Manley and the PNP. Consequently, he acquired the nickname "Joshua", after the biblical figure, and also a rod to symbolize leading the people into the Promised Land. Stone (1992) described the use of these symbols as "symbolic manipulation". In the context of political communication, these symbols are used to transfer meaning of power and authority. They were also used to connect the leader to the citizens, as Jamaica has a strong Christian population who readily identified with such symbolism. It must also be noted that in the context of political communication, music played a pivotal role in the transference of messages to citizens.

Both Manley and Shearer traversed the length and breadth of the country marketing their political campaign messages. They were both articulate platform speakers, and they used this talent as a means to convey their messages. Indeed, at the time, the presence of television was not strong on the island. JBC TV was the only television station, and it was owned and operated by the government. As a result, there was greater dependence on face-to-face communication through groups and branches, as well as radio and newspapers, to transmit messages. Manley and the PNP emerged victorious in the elections that were held on 29 February. With a voter turnout of 78.2 per cent, the PNP won thirty-seven of the fifty-three available seats, while the JLP won sixteen (ECJ 1972).

At the heart of this campaign were the leaders of the political parties, driving their campaign messages among citizens. Manley had tapped into popular discontent in the public sphere and used that to formulate his message, using the group structures of the PNP to mobilize support in the communities across the island. Intrinsic to this was feedback from the communities through the groups, which redounded to his political success. He was also seen as a charming and handsome man; this presentation created a very good television image, especially to women. These factors all contributed to his victory.

The 1976 Election

The 1976 election was regarded as one of the most controversial in the history of Jamaica. This was because it was held during a time when the country was under a state of emergency, and a number of prominent leaders from the opposition JLP were being detained by the security forces. The JLP believed that this situation contributed to its defeat. However, this view was strongly rejected by the Manley-led PNP administration.

The 1976 election came within the context of a plethora of challenges and achievements during Manley's administration. Upon assuming the office of prime minister in 1972, he introduced a compendia of programmes, policies and legislation to assist in changing the economic and social landscape of the country. Some of these have been articulated earlier in this book. However, it must be noted that they formed the basis of the Manley-led PNP campaign of 1976. For example, take one of the most popular songs to be developed by the party – "The Message" – penned by Neville Martin. The lyrics highlighted some of the achievements of the PNP since 1972:

My fada born yah,
My fada born yah,
My granmada born yah,
My granmada born yah,

I man I born yah,
I man I born yah.
My leada born yah,
My leada born yah,
Das why I nah lef yah,
No I nah lef yah.
He gave I a message,
To all those people,
Who nuh love progress,
Who nuh love progress.
He say to jook dem with Land Lease,
Jook dem wid Land Lease,
Den yuh jook dem wid di Pioneer Corp,
Jook dem wid Pioneer Corp,
Jook dem wid JAMAL,
Jook dem wid JAMAL,
den yuh jook dem wid Free Education,
Jook dem wid Free Education,
Equal pay for women,
Equal pay for women,
Jook dem wid di Minimum Wage,
Jook dem wid di Minimum Wage.
My leada born yah,
My leada born yah,
Suh help mi God I nah lef yah,
No I nah lef yah.
Mi a satta wid discipline,
Under heavy, heavy manners,
Mi in a di struggle to,
Mi in a di struggle to.
No Bastard nuh deh again,
No Bastard nuh deh again,
Everyone lawful,
Woe uh woe, everyone lawful . . .

In the meantime, the JLP had undergone another leadership change in 1974, and Seaga emerged as its new leader. He had been minister of finance and development under both the Bustamante and the Shearer regimes of the 1960s. He had developed a reputation for fiscal prudence as he had presided over the period of growth in the 1960s.

Seaga pitched the JLP's campaign on the economic challenges being experienced in Jamaica and posited the view that Manley was taking the country on the wrong ideological path. His arguments were made in the context of the compendium of social programmes that were being implemented and the fact that the economy was not growing enough to fund them. Seaga also believed that the policies of the PNP were hostile to private capital, contributed to the commencement of capital flight, and were laying the foundation for the introduction of communism (Panton 1993; Seaga 2009).

For the PNP, the campaign in 1976 took shape at the annual conference in September. Estimates indicated that over twenty-five thousand people attended, and the meeting which had been scheduled for the National Arena had to be transferred to the National Stadium. At that meeting, Manley gave one of his seminal political speeches: "We are not for sale." He launched a verbal assault on local and international groups that he described as "cliques", accusing them of joining forces to undermine his administration. The speech was recorded on vinyl and cassette and was distributed islandwide to members and supporters of the PNP, and along with the song "The Message", was used to mobilize citizens at PNP campaign meetings. It must be noted that it was the first time in a political campaign in Jamaica that the popular reggae rhythm was used to put the message of a political leader and party to music and communicate with the electorate. This was a fundamental political communication development in Jamaica.

After months of intense campaigning, the PNP emerged victorious in the December election. Voter turnout was 84.5 per cent. The number of constituencies was increased from fifty-three in 1972 to sixty in 1976 and the PNP won forty-seven seats to the JLP's thirteen (ECJ 1972, 1976).

Manley was returned as prime minister for a second term. Again, there was strong evidence that leader-centric political campaigning was intrinsic in Jamaica. As presented in the models of communication designed by Lasswell and Hall and his colleagues, there must be a driving force behind the message for it to be seen as credible. Both Manley and Seaga were dominant forces in the conceptualization and marketing of the messages of their political organizations.

The 1980 Election

In 1980, the Seaga-led JLP defeated the PNP after a bitter election. The elections came in the context of growing economic challenges after the country terminated its borrowing relationship with the IMF in 1979, and violence between rivalling members of the leading political parties intensified. According to

Prime Minister Michael Manley, the elections were called to get a new mandate from the people in an effort to relax some of the political tensions in the society.

The elections were announced in Montego Bay (Sam Sharpe Square), to tremendous fanfare, in February. This set the stage for a very long campaign (eight months) and contributed to the significant levels of violence that were experienced in the lead-up to the voting. The election was fought over three main issues: economic policy, social policy and ideology.

The Seaga-led JLP hinged its electoral fortunes on the country's bad economic state. They charged that the Manley-led PNP had mismanaged the nation's resources, and that this resulted in the end of its borrowing relationship with the IMF. The JLP further charged that it was Manley's fault that the borrowing relationship had come to a halt, the suggestion being that Manley's team had been unable to meet the agreed targets. Consequently, the Seaga team coined a new interpretation of the acronym *IMF*: "It's Manley's Fault".

Recognizing the economic challenges and the fact that the Jamaican society was caught in an ideological stalemate, the JLP pitched its campaign around the economy. They strongly advocated for the establishment of a free market economy, in which the private sector would control the engines of production. They pledged to Jamaicans that the establishment of this system of economic management would ensure "dunnie [money] would jingle in the pockets".

This advocacy of a free market system attracted huge support from the private sector. A number of businessmen funded and organized activities for the Seaga-led JLP, and they were even accused by the PNP of sabotaging the ruling Manley administration. The accusation widened the gap between the PNP and the Private Sector Organisation of Jamaica. According to Ronald Sasso, a prominent Jamaican businessman, the government was giving politics priority over production. With great passion, Sasso expressed the views of the private sector at the time – there was a great deal of obsession with politics, and this was impeding the development of the country.

The social agenda also figured prominently in the campaign. It was the major issue that the Manley administration had campaigned on. During the 1970s, it had introduced a number of social programmes geared to transforming society. The programmes and policies were immensely popular with Jamaicans, especially women and young people. Some of these programmes included free education, JAMAL, the NYS, maternity leave with pay, free health care and the National Housing Trust. These, the PNP claimed, would be abolished by the JLP if they were given the opportunity to govern the country.

The year 1980 constituted the height of this ideological divide. It saw Jamaican society plunge into crisis because the major political parties were deep in the defence of their ideological positions. This was further aggravated by the levels of support given by countries outside Jamaica. On the one hand, the USSR and Cuba were providing strong support to the PNP, and on the other, the United States and Britain were giving similar support to the JLP. Support hinged on the control of states based on their ideological posture. The United States was bent on repelling any attempts to establish another communist state on its doorstep, and in an effort to preserve the Monroe Doctrine, they moved aggressively to ensure that Manley was defeated by Seaga. Ostensibly, the JLP received funding from private US-based organizations as well as from local entrepreneurs who embraced the capitalist philosophy. The JLP, therefore, had significant cash that could be used to enhance its organizational efforts and finance its media campaign.

Some Jamaicans had a deep-seated fear that if the PNP returned to office, communism would be introduced and they would lose their freedom. Seaga, as an anthropologist, knew the value that Jamaicans placed on freedom. According to Patterson, this argument was deliberately designed to invoke fear in the minds of Jamaican citizens. In the context of political communication, the introduction of fear into political campaigning is a propaganda technique to attract voters, especially those who have doubts about particular issues. Lippmann (2004, 28) stated, "In order to conduct propaganda, there must be some barrier between the public and the event." Lippmann was the first intellectual to develop a theoretical framework around the issue of propaganda, through his books *Public Opinion* and *Phantom Public*, even though it was the Germans who perfected the practice in the First World War. Walther Schulze-Wechsungen, former head of the district propaganda office of the Propaganda Ministry Berlin-Brandenburg, sought to draw a distinction between political propaganda and advertisement. He stated: "Advertising is promotion for something physical, indeed for something specific. Advertising serves the economy, or particular areas, purposes and tasks. Advertising praises goods. Propaganda spreads an idea. Propaganda serves only politics" (Schulze-Wechsungen 1934, 7).

Schulze-Wechsungen (1934, 8) further argued: "Naturally the propagandist must understand not only the means that are at his disposal, but also the characteristics of 'his' masses, however they are expressed, of whatever type they may be. The enemy may command better resources, and will certainly take pleasure and satisfaction in any mistake. He will exploit any failure."

The JLP repeated the argument of the PNP introducing communism so frequently that it became a truism in Jamaican society. In the context of political propaganda, the repetition of a message is important to solicit the support of voters.

Seaga understood the political culture of the Jamaican people. Through its branches and other affiliated groups, the JLP embarked on an intense propaganda campaign which revolved largely around ideology: the central message revolved around the alleged intent by the PNP to introduce communism in Jamaica. But the PNP was not daunted by the propaganda onslaught. Instead, it relied heavily on Cuba and the USSR to assist in countering the pressure that was being brought to bear on the administration because of its adherence to democratic socialism (Panton 1993).

The PNP also had its propaganda strategy. Through its groups, members of the organization were indoctrinated in the values of democratic socialism. They were informed that if the JLP won the election, the social gains of the 1970s would be dismantled.

While the PNP received assistance from socialist governments overseas, the resources were insignificant compared to those of the JLP. As a result, the PNP had to rely heavily on controlled, state-run machinery. This too had its challenges because there were public officials caught in the ideological divide, and this had serious implications for the implementation of state-run programmes and policies.

The three issues outlined here set the stage for an intriguing media campaign. All the available media houses were vehicles of intense advertising and propaganda campaigns. Talk shows on the radio were the source of daily political attacks. Talk show hosts were all labelled and placed in political camps of one sort or the other. Members of the political parties would call the radio stations on a daily basis, advocating for the various issues articulated by their party leaders. Special individuals were trained by the political parties to call in to talk shows and deliver particular messages relating to their positions.

The leaders of political parties competed heavily for air time, as they made intense efforts to have their views and messages broadcast to citizens. It was the same in the print media. The two paramount newspapers, the *Daily Gleaner* and the *Daily News,* were both accused of being partisan. The *Daily Gleaner* was said to be aligned with the JLP and therefore pro-Seaga, while the *Daily News* was accused of being pro-Manley and supportive of the PNP. Stone (1981, 8) penned:

> The mass media played a major role in the campaign. The government-owned radio and television station, the Jamaica Broadcasting Corporation and the government-owned *Daily News* newspaper projected a heavy leftist PNP line in news presentations and commentary. On the other hand, the privately owned *Daily Gleaner* newspaper was equally pro-JLP and anti-PNP in its commentary. The government-owned radio station, Radio Jamaica, tended to hold the scales evenly between the parties in presenting news, although some of its commentary was slanted in favour of the PNP.

Both political parties advertised heavily in the media. However, because of the significant funding the JLP received from local private-sector and overseas organizations and individuals, they were able to gain greater visibility. Meanwhile, the PNP relied heavily on the Agency for Public Information. This was the official information arm of the government, and so it was entitled to a certain amount of air time on radio and television. The government used this mechanism to promote its implemented programmes and policies. Simultaneously, the PNP produced a monthly newsletter called the *Rising Sun* to promote its programmes and policies to its members and supporters across the island. The Workers Party of Jamaica, which was a communist-oriented political organization and a PNP sympathizer, also produced a newsletter called *Struggle* which was also circulated nationally and was vehement in its opposition to capitalist policies.

Both political parties produced campaign songs using the reggae rhythm. The JLP produced a song entitled "Palms of Victory, Bells Are Freedom", while the PNP produced a song entitled "Stand Firm". These songs formed a considerable part of the propaganda artillery of the parties and were geared towards mobilizing party supporters, capitalizing on the increasingly popular reggae, which was now an entrenched part of the cultural landscape of Jamaica. Here again, we see popular culture being blended into national politics as a means of marketing the message of political parties.

On the streets of the nation, both political parties took their message to the people in the towns and villages. The national campaigns merged with the local campaigns for political parties in the communities, and this contributed to extensive conflicts. In the public sphere, the political parties were locked in an ideological battle. During this time, guns and ammunition were given to young men to defend their political party, which contributed to the death of over eight hundred Jamaicans in the lead-up to the elections.

The JLP campaigned under the theme "Deliverance". This was linked to the economic hardship that Jamaicans were experiencing and the argument of rescuing the country from communism (Engels 2013). Conversely, the PNP campaigned on the slogan "Standing firm for a third term", as it was seeking its third consecutive term and holding to its democratic socialist principles.

The leadership of both pre-eminent political parties could be seen and felt in nearly every community islandwide. According to Seaga, Shearer, the deputy leader of the JLP, was extremely influential by providing him with support in the field. Shearer was president general of the Bustamante Industrial Trade Union, which gave him a popular platform on which to campaign with the working class. These efforts were further supported by Bruce Golding, general secretary of the party, a young, bright man who was instrumental in mobilizing the youth. Combined, Seaga, Shearer and Golding presented a potent and united team to Jamaicans.

In the interim, the PNP was undergoing challenges. Manley had Patterson as his deputy, and D.K. Duncan was the general secretary. The PNP was embroiled in deep internal organizational struggles and conflict involving three dominant factions: those on the right, those at the centre and those who were leftist in their political orientation. This made it difficult for individuals to work together and ultimately contributed to the defeat of the PNP on 30 October 1980. Wherever there are serious internal divisions in a political organization, the message will be affected. This is what transpired with the PNP in 1980. With a voter turnout of 86.1 per cent, the JLP won fifty-one of the available sixty seats to the PNP's nine, and up to that time, it was the most convincing electoral victory for any political party in Jamaica.

The 1983 Election

The second national election won by the JLP under the leadership of Seaga occurred in 1983. Seaga's popularity had diminished between 1980 and 1983 due to a series of harsh measures that his administration implemented, and he was perceived by Jamaicans as being an autocratic leader. But his electoral victory came within the context of the Grenada invasion by the United States. Once again, the JLP was positioned such that it had a distinct opportunity over the PNP. It was strongly believed that the organizers of the coup that led to the overthrow of the prime mnister, Maurice Bishop, was about to introduce communism in Grenada. The United States would have no new communist state established on its doorstep, so it invaded the country to prevent that possibility. Seaga was the point man in the Caribbean, tasked to take charge of the operation. As discussed in chapter 6, he helped mobilize Caribbean troops, and this had a positive effect on his political stock in Jamaica. At that time, public opinion polls had shown his JLP trailing the PNP, but his involvement in the US-led invasion clearly assisted in bolstering his chances. So a confident Seaga called snap elections for December 1983.

The PNP decided not to contest the elections (as explained further in chapter 4), citing an agreement between the parties to withhold elections until the electoral system was reformed, including checking the existing voters' list. Snap elections constituted a breach of that accord. But because it was basically a gentleman's agreement between Manley and Seaga, it had no legal grounding. The JLP went ahead with the uncontested elections, and for the first time in Jamaica's modern political history, Parliament was totally controlled by a single political party (table 1). All sixty seats in the House of Representative were occupied by the Seaga-led JLP. Nevertheless, Seaga used the opportunity to ask the governor general, Sir Florizel Glasspole, to appoint eight independent senators

Table 1. Election Outcomes by Constituencies in 1980 and 1983

Constituencies	1980	1983
East Rural St Andrew	JLP	JLP
East St Andrew	JLP	JLP
North-Central St Andrew	JLP	JLP
North-West St Andrew	JLP	JLP
West Rural St Andrew	JLP	JLP
Western St Andrew	PNP	JLP
West-Central St Andrew	JLP	JLP
East-Central St Andrew	PNP	JLP
South-West St Andrew	PNP	JLP
South-East St Andrew	JLP	JLP
South St Andrew	PNP	JLP
West Kingston	JLP	JLP
West-Central Kingston	PNP	JLP
East-Central Kingston	PNP	JLP
East Kingston and Port Royal	JLP	JLP
West St Thomas	JLP	JLP
Eastern St Thomas	JLP	JLP
East Portland	JLP	JLP
West Portland	JLP	JLP
South-East St Mary	JLP	JLP
East-Central St Mary	PNP	JLP
West-Central St Mary	PNP	JLP
West St Mary	JLP	JLP
South-East St Ann	PNP	JLP
North-East St Ann	JLP	JLP
North-West St Ann	JLP	JLP
South-West St Ann	JLP	JLP
North Trelawny	JLP	JLP
South Trelawny	JLP	JLP
East-Central St James	JLP	JLP
West-Central St James	JLP	JLP
North-West St James	JLP	JLP
South St James	JLP	JLP
East Hanover	JLP	JLP
West Hanover	JLP	JLP
West Westmoreland	JLP	JLP
Central Westmoreland	JLP	JLP
North-East Westmoreland	JLP	JLP
South-East Westmoreland	JLP	JLP
North-West St Elizabeth	JLP	JLP

(*Continued*)

Table 1. (*continued*)

Constituencies	1980	1983
North-East St Elizabeth	JLP	JLP
South-West St Elizabeth	JLP	JLP
South-East St Elizabeth	JLP	JLP
South Manchester	JLP	JLP
Central Manchester	JLP	JLP
North-West Manchester	JLP	JLP
North-East Manchester	JLP	JLP
North-West Clarendon	JLP	JLP
North Clarendon	JLP	JLP
North-Central Clarendon	JLP	JLP
Central Clarendon	JLP	JLP
South-West Clarendon	JLP	JLP
South-East Clarendon	JLP	JLP
South-West St Catherine	JLP	JLP
South-East St Catherine	JLP	JLP
North-West St Catherine	JLP	JLP
North-East St Catherine	JLP	JLP
West-Central St Catherine	JLP	JLP
East-Central St Catherine	JLP	JLP
South-Central St Catherine	JLP	JLP

Source: ECJ (1980, 1983).

as a means of providing oversight to the operations of the government and to preserve the democratic institutions. These eight senators were Lloyd Barnett, Courtney Fletcher, Clarence Reid, Charles Sinclair, Emil George, Errol Miller, Barbara Blake-Hannah and Keith Worrell.

In analysing the election of 1983, Seaga claimed that he was provoked by a challenge from Paul Robertson, general secretary of the PNP, who issued a call for Seaga to resign as minister of finance. This call aggravated Seaga and contributed to his calling the snap election (Seaga 2009).

The 1989 Election

The next national election called by Seaga in his capacity as prime minister was in 1989, after five years of JLP hegemony in the House of Representatives. The PNP decided to contest the elections this time around.

Seaga's popularity had declined by this time, as citizens perceived him as an uncaring and autocratic leader. This was evidenced in several instances, including the reduction of many social programmes. Retrenchment of the public service was based on the policy recommendations of the IMF, but citizens perceived that Seaga was the man behind the policies, so they were frustrated with him. The Manley-led PNP also linked these hardships to Seaga, and citizens bought the message.

Another instance of lack of caring was related to Hurricane Gilbert, which hit the island in 1988. Most citizens were disgusted by the way that benefits for relief were handled – especially the distribution of zinc sheets for the repair of roofs. People felt that that was being done on a partisan basis, so they felt that the JLP had to go ("Partisan Zinc Hand-Outs Alleged", *Daily Gleaner*, 29 August 1989).

Stone (1989a, 178) best summarized the situation relating to Seaga, stating the following:

> Edward Seaga did not communicate in a style and language that the people understood. When he spoke, few Jamaicans took the trouble to listen as he bored them with details and statistics. He behaved like an authoritarian colonial governor and inspired fear rather than love and admiration. He failed either to mobilize the energies and loyalties of the Jamaican people owing to his technocratic leadership style or to convince the masses that he was carrying out necessary austerity adjustments to the economy as against simply ignoring the needs of the poor and catering to capital, businessmen, investors, the rich and the middle class.

The PNP had undergone significant rebranding in the meantime. Recognizing the fallout from its democratic socialist past and close flirtations with communist states, the Manley-led PNP took certain strategic decisions designed to present itself as a reformed political organization. They got rid of prominent officials within its ranks, such as Anthony Spaulding and D.K. Duncan, who had strong leanings to the left, and revised their position on the approach needed to manage the economy. In the same place, Stone stated:

> Manley was no longer talking the language of a firebrand and radical leftist as in the 1970s. He no longer even used the word socialism. His new image was that of a caring, concerned, sober and statesmanlike leader who was committed to easing the burdens imposed on the poorer classes by the Seaga government. He would put people first compared with Seaga's prior emphasis on fiscal and financial prudence. How he planned to do this was never made clear but the new Manley image was seductive and overwhelming after eight years of impersonal technocratic government by Edward Seaga whose political style alienated many Jamaican voters.

The PNP outlined to the public their administration's willingness to allow the private sector to play the lead role in the economy, while the government would confine itself to ensuring the adequacy of social services. The party, therefore, was able to attract financial support from members of the private sector once again.

The PNP hinged its 1989 election campaign on the country's growing debt problem and the dismantling of social services by the JLP administration. As previously noted, it had as its campaign theme "We put people first", while the JLP countered with its campaign slogan "It takes cash to care". These two distinctly different slogans reflected the philosophical positions of both political parties. The PNP slogan indicated an approach of involving the people, regardless of the availability of money. The JLP's, on the other hand, reflected its conservative values and the need for money to implement programmes and policies.

The media was again required to play a major role in the 1989 elections. However, this time, the balance of power had shifted and more media houses supported the new approach of Manley and the PNP. Moreover, the world was experiencing rapid changes in geopolitics as communism was being dismantled in Europe and Asia. The PNP approach helped temper the ideological division that existed in society, and it had a ripple effect on the media.

The PNP had also gone through a restructuring of its organization, and the groups which constituted its base support were functioning more effectively. Robertson, a former lecturer in the Department of Government at the University of the West Indies, had taken over the responsibility of general secretary from Duncan in 1983. Various members of the PNP credited Robertson for the restructuring that took place during the 1980s, which contributed to the PNP's success in the election.

Ironically, the Seaga-led JLP was not as organized as they were in 1980. The arms and affiliates that were instrumental in that election victory had fallen into abeyance. According to Bruce Golding, eight years of consecutive governmental involvement had led to their neglect and caused the JLP to lose organizational focus on the ground. Moreover, Seaga himself had become the central factor in the organization, which contributed to the demise of the branches. All major decisions relating to the JLP revolved around Seaga. That year, the PNP ended up winning the 1989 elections, capturing forty-five of the sixty seats in Parliament to the JLP's fifteen, with a voter turnout of 77.59 per cent (ECJ 1989). Michael Manley once again returned to lead the country as prime minister, with Patterson as his deputy.

In table 2, some cases of elections and results from the 1989 and 1993 elections are examined. It is clear from the information provided that the Seaga-led administration had some challenges communicating its programmes and policies to Jamaican citizens and converting them into electoral victory in 1989 and 1993.

Table 2. Election Outcomes by Constituencies in 1989 and 1993

Constituency	1989	1993
East Rural St Andrew	PNP	PNP
East St Andrew	JLP	PNP
East-Central St Andrew	PNP	PNP
North-East St Andrew	N/A	PNP
North-Central St Andrew	JLP	PNP
North-West St Andrew	JLP	JLP
South-East St Andrew	PNP	PNP
South-West St Andrew	PNP	PNP
South St Andrew	PNP	PNP
*West Rural St Andrew	PNP	PNP
West-Central St Andrew	PNP	PNP
West St Andrew	PNP	PNP
East Kingston and Port Royal	PNP	PNP
Central Kingston	PNP	PNP
West Kingston	JLP	JLP
West St Thomas	JLP	PNP
East St Thomas	JLP	PNP
East Portland	PNP	PNP
West Portland	PNP	PNP
South-East St Mary	PNP	PNP
Central St Mary	PNP	PNP
West St Mary	PNP	PNP
*North-East St Ann	PNP	PNP
*North-West St Ann	PNP	PNP
South-East St Ann	PNP	PNP
South-West St Ann	JLP	JLP
North Trelawny	PNP	PNP
South Trelawny	JLP	PNP
*East-Central St James	PNP	PNP
*West-Central St James	PNP	PNP
*North-West St James	PNP	PNP
South St James	PNP	PNP
East Hanover	PNP	PNP
West Hanover	PNP	PNP
West Westmoreland	PNP	PNP
Central Westmoreland	PNP	PNP
North-East Westmoreland	PNP	N/A
South-East Westmoreland	PNP	PNP
North-West St Elizabeth	JLP	PNP
North-East St Elizabeth	PNP	PNP

(*Continued*)

Table 2. (*continued*)

Constituency	1989	1993
South-East St Elizabeth	PNP	PNP
South-West St Elizabeth	PNP	PNP
South Manchester	PNP	PNP
Central Manchester	PNP	PNP
North-West Manchester	PNP	PNP
North-East Manchester	PNP	JLP
North-West Clarendon	PNP	PNP
North Clarendon	PNP	PNP
North-Central Clarendon	JLP	PNP
Central Clarendon	JLP	JLP
South-East Clarendon	JLP	PNP
South-West Clarendon	PNP	PNP
North-West St Catherine	PNP	PNP
North-East St Catherine	JLP	PNP
East-Central St Catherine	PNP	PNP
West-Central St Catherine	JLP	JLP
Central St Catherine	JLP	JLP
South-West St Catherine	PNP	PNP
South-Central St Catherine	PNP	PNP
South-East St Catherine	PNP	PNP
South St Catherine	PNP	PNP

Source: ECJ (1989, 1993).

*Note that boundary changes were made in St Mary, Westmoreland, Kingston and St Catherine in the two elections. In the 1989 election, the constituencies were reduced to three in St Mary and two in Kingston; these were added to St Catherine. In the 1993 election, the number of constituencies in Westmoreland was reduced to three and one was added to St Andrew (North-East St Andrew).

In the two elections that it won in 1980 and 1983, foreign affairs and foreign policy played a quintessential role in determining the outcome. Jamaicans were obviously fearful of the introduction of communism at home, as well as in any other state close to its borders. Jamaicans had long relished their freedom, and this is best captured in a statement made by one of its national heroes, Sam Sharpe, "I would rather die upon yonder gallows, than to live in slavery" – a perfect testament to the intrinsic value of freedom. As a person who studied local culture, specifically the Maroons, Seaga understood this and successfully linked it to the perception that Manley was a communist.

By 1989, however, communism was in decline all over the world, so there was little fear in society about this system of government. Moreover, the PNP had undergone some reform of its ideological posturing, which also helped to minimize communist perception within society. Consequently, it was able to market itself as a credible alternative to the JLP and set the stage for political dominance over the next two decades.

After Michael Manley returned to power in 1989, the PNP embarked on a programme of economic liberalization. This new approach was an attempt to convince society of its reforms and to inspire confidence among the private sector. One institution to undergo significant reform was the media. As indicated in chapter 2, prior to 1989, there were just four radio stations, one major newspaper and one television station. The media landscape, therefore, was closed in the context of free market ideology. The Manley regime commenced the process of liberalizing the industry, and this started the metamorphosis in the media landscape.

In 1992, Manley communicated his intention to retire from active politics, and Patterson emerged as his successor after an intense internal election campaign. Patterson defeated Portia Simpson for the presidency of the PNP. His victory came in the wake of his resignation in 1991 as minister of finance and planning and that of his cabinet colleague, Horace Clarke, over the issuance of a special waiver to a corporate company. However, following the political firestorm which it triggered and Patterson's departure, he made what became a famous statement in the Jamaican political landscape: "I shall return."

While out of the cabinet, he took the opportunity to reinvent himself as he planned to assume leadership of the PNP. He had received information in January 1992 of Manley's failing health, and his peers decided that he should make himself available to replace him. Patterson signalled his intent to run for the party leadership in February 1992 and galvanized a high-powered campaign team which included Clarke, Maxine Henry-Wilson, Vincent "Vin" Lawrence and other influential members of the PNP. According to Clarke, the campaign was gruelling, but Patterson secured 2,322 of the delegate votes, while Simpson secured 756.

The 1993 Election

With the internal party elections out of the way and Patterson now leading the party and the government, he put together his cabinet, which included Simpson and other members of her team who had campaigned against him. This was an important gesture because the PNP's success at the polls depended on unity within the organization. As a seasoned political campaigner, Patterson understood this reality. He immediately signalled his intention to seek his own mandate, but this was not to happen until the economic liberalization programme which commenced under Manley was accelerated (Patterson 2018).

The media was again the focus, and this resulted in its expansion in the early 1990s. By 2002, the sector included approximately eighteen radio stations, three national television stations, three major newspapers, over forty cable providers and widespread use of the Internet (PIOJ 2002). This is extremely important so as to contextualize the Patterson era. It was during this period of media expansion that a fertile foundation was laid for the practice of political communication in Jamaica.

Accepting the reins of power of the PNP and Jamaica from the charismatic Michael Manley meant that the calm and technocratic Patterson had to carve out his own niche. Patterson claimed he realized the need to establish his own style of communicating with the Jamaican people, as this would be essential for his success. Consequently, he immediately established the Live and Direct and the Face-to-Face initiatives, which would see both him and his ministers communicating directly with the people.

According to Patterson, when he assumed leadership of the PNP and the country, there were individuals who claimed that the party did not have a chance to win an election against the JLP with him at the helm. This was placed in two contexts – the first had to do with events prior to his assumption of leadership, such as his resignation in 1991 and accusations of corruption. The second issue concerned the economic liberalization programme of the PNP-led administration, which adversely affected citizens' quality of life. Basic items frequently consumed by the poor were no longer being subsidized. The Jamaican currency was depreciating at a rapid rate, and inflation had increased significantly, hovering at approximately 80 per cent (PIOJ 1993). These cumulative factors had a negative impact on citizens and the public opinion polls were showing declining fortunes for the PNP. Political scientists had little hope for a Patterson victory. But he claimed that he had used his hiatus from the cabinet to travel the country and touch base with delegates of the PNP in preparation for his appointment with destiny. He did indeed defy all odds.

Coincidentally, during the same period that the PNP was transitioning, a fracas emerged in the JLP. A group of senior officials were demanding the resignation of Seaga, as they thought it was time for him to go. Seaga overheard the murmurings, and the matter plunged the JLP into a political leadership crisis. Included in the quarrel were officials such as Pearnel Charles, Edmund Bartlett and Karl Samuda. They left the JLP, and Samuda eventually crossed the floor of Parliament, becoming a member of the PNP.

Without hesitation, Patterson seized the initiative and called an election. The political pendulum swung strongly in his favour, which could be attributed to four main factors:

- The ongoing imbroglio in the JLP caused the party to be viewed by voters as a disunited political organization that was not prepared for governance.
- The matter of race was brought to the forefront. Patterson is a black Jamaican, and citizens readily identified with him. Moreover, Seaga, a white Jamaican, referred to Patterson as a "black scandal-bag" at a public meeting. Not surprisingly, the utterance were not well received by the population and came back to haunt him. The PNP used the racist slur in various campaigns against Seaga and the JLP, intensifying its inappropriateness in multiple advertisements.
- Patterson's introduction of Live and Direct in 1992 was another influence. Patterson understood the importance of the prime minister having one-on-one communications with citizens. Live and Direct was developed as a tool whereby the prime minister went into communities to discuss matters of national importance on a quarterly basis, and it was supported by another communication strategy, Face-to-Face. This allowed members of the cabinet and members of Parliament to interface regularly with constituencies on matters relating to their ministerial portfolios and constituencies. These two communication mechanisms proved to be very effective, as citizens attended the multiple town halls to interact with their leaders.
- Finally, the organizational strength of the Patterson-led PNP was a major contributor to its good fortune. The PNP had just emerged from a special conference to elect a new leader. The groups that formed the base of the PNP had been activated, and the members on the ground were energized. There were over 3,800 groups, with membership of approximately forty thousand loyal supporters. Upon Patterson's convincing win over Simpson, a senior vice president and cabinet minister, as leader, he reappointed all the ministers who had supported her to positions in the government. This attempt to preserve the unity of the PNP undoubtedly facilitated the healing process and enabled it to face the electorate more quickly than had been anticipated.

According to Patterson, the campaign atmosphere for the PNP was fertile. With the JLP in turmoil and the PNP just returning from its special conference, the environment was ripe for campaigning (P.J. Patterson, personal communication). With this in mind, the PNP was poised for victory.

As pointed out earlier in this chapter, the media was undergoing extensive changes as well, as more television and radio stations populated the landscape. The atmosphere was being transformed into a competitive arena in which media houses had to compete for news. In this context, the coverage of political party events increased. Additionally, more advertising was released, as the two major political parties made a gallant effort to communicate their messages to the public. Ultimately, the Patterson-led PNP emerged victorious, winning fifty-two of the sixty seats. The voter turnout of 66.74 per cent (ECJ 1993). This was the largest victory recorded for any political party in Jamaica.

The 1997 Election

The next election for the Patterson administration was 1997. This election also came at a time when the country was experiencing significant challenges, especially in the financial sector. As pointed out in chapter 4, the financial sector had collapsed after a number of the indigenous banks encountered serious liquidity problems and eventually folded. The government had decided to bail out some of these institutions.

According to Patterson (personal communication), "this had to be done in order to preserve social stability". He submitted further that at a Live and Direct meeting in Trelawny, citizens clearly expressed to him the social consequences of them not being able to retrieve their hard-earned money deposited in the banks. Therefore, he and his administration had no choice but to give support to the financial sector so that the small account holders "could collect their money" (Patterson, personal communication).

While all of this was happening, Golding, a senior official in the JLP, resigned and formed the National Democratic Movement (NDM). This new political party was established in 1995 on a platform hinged on constitutional reform. Golding claimed that he had done so against a background of being "fed up" with tribal politics and the need to be a part of a new wind of change within the country. Golding had developed serious difficulties with Seaga after being accused of being a member of the so-called Gang of Five which wanted to force Seaga into retirement. Once again, the JLP was plunged into turmoil; their chaos was not attractive to the electorate.

At the same time, Samuda resigned from the PNP and rejoined the JLP. This move was to become a vital part of the election as the PNP established its media campaign.

The issue of political advertising and campaigning took on renewed significance in the 1990s as competition in the media intensified. It also came against the background of an increasing decline in the voter population as apathy among the electorate increased. The political parties were thus forced to advertise aggressively to win the hearts and minds of the electorate. All the political parties put advertisements in the varied news media. However, the advertisement that appealed most to voters was that which the PNP initiated, featuring Samuda. It highlighted a speech which was given by Samuda at one of the PNP's annual conferences, where he was heard denouncing Seaga and the JLP. This was replayed in an advertisement entitled "Cock Mouth Kill Cock".

The advertisement proved to be a game changer and played a pivotal role in the demise of the JLP in that election. Citizens were reminded of Samuda's rhetoric after resigning from the JLP in 1992. The PNP won the election by a significant majority in 1997, capturing fifty out of the possible sixty seats. The voter turnout was 65.22 per cent (ECJ 1997).

The margin of victory for the PNP in the 1997 election consolidated the view that once an administration had an effective communication programme, it was likely to appeal successfully to the voting public. Between 1993 and 1997, the communication strategies of the Patterson administration continued to peak, and this had a positive effect for the PNP in winning votes. The Live and Direct and the Face-to-Face features were seen and heard islandwide. It is estimated that between 1993 and 1997, there were over one hundred Live and Direct and Face-to-Face presentations. Also, the organizational machinery of the PNP was strong, as they were still benefiting from the leadership transition which had taken place in 1992, as well as the appointment of a new general secretary, Maxine Henry-Wilson, in 1994.

The 2002 Election

The 2002 election was one of the most intriguing that has ever been contested in Jamaica, and it resulted in the narrowest victory ever in the nation. The PNP was campaigning for its fourth successive victory, and the Seaga-led JLP was seeking its first win since 1989.

The election campaign of 2002 can be easily described as one of the most modern in the political landscape of Jamaica. It was the first time that the Internet and information technology played a considerable role in any campaign on the island. This occurred in the context of the liberalization of the telecommunications sector after a fifty-year licence had been granted to the Jamaica Telecommunications Company in 1988. This licence gave the company a monopoly on all telecommunications services. The policy decision contributed to poor service to citizens and limited citizens' access to what was becoming an increasingly important sector within the economy. The legislation governing the monopoly telecommunication company was thereafter repealed, and a new Telecommunications Act was put into effect, as well as a new tele-communications policy outlining the Patterson administration's position on this sector, which was tabled in Parliament in 1998.

As a result of this liberalization, competition became the new order of business. A number of new entrants were now providing a compendium of services to citizens. The introduction of the Internet and cellular phones was critical to this effort. By 2002, there were approximately 250,000 individuals in the island with access to the Internet; over 400,000 had landline telephones, and approximately 1.2 million had cellular phones (PIOJ 2002).

The new environment provided an interesting landscape for the election campaign of 2002. The PNP hinged its campaign on the modernizing of Jamaica's infrastructure through the introduction of modern means of tele-communications, so it labelled its campaign "Log On to Progress". Conversely, the JLP campaigned on issues relating to mismanagement and corruption in the Patterson administration, as well as on education.

There were a number of allegations of corrupt practices by ministers associated with the administration. Of notable significance were allegations of corruption in Operation PRIDE and the Info-Tech Fund – two far-reaching programmes implemented by the Patterson administration.

The expanded media landscape provided maximum coverage of the election campaign for both political organizations. Political rallies were broadcast live and brought the campaigns into citizens' homes. Again, this was made possible because a significant portion of the Jamaican population now had access to their own radio and television sets. According to STATIN (2002), approximately 70 per cent of the population had access to these media, with 2.5 million radios and approximately 1.6 million television sets on the island by 2002.

To some degree, advertisement took on a renewed significance in the media; the art and science of political communication became evident. Both political parties demonstrated their creative energies by capitalizing on the perceived mistakes of the opposing side. These were subsequently displayed in multiple advertisements, and in this context, there were two that inspired very positive responses for both parties.

The first, created by the JLP, featured Patterson singing Frank Sinatra's "My Way" at his seventieth birthday party. They linked the collapse of a bridge in a rural constituency to the song and showed the bridge collapsing while Patterson was singing. The JLP tried to convey through this depiction that the problems that the country was facing at the time were a direct result of Patterson's stubbornness.

The second, for the PNP, showed a known JLP leader, Christopher Tufton, making a public pronouncement upon his return to that political organization. Instead of requesting supporters to vote for the "bell" (the symbol for the JLP), he admonished them to vote for the "head", the symbol for the PNP. This advertisement came out the day after the statement was made.

These advertisements demonstrate the intensity of the campaign of 2002, which can be attributed to three factors. First, the media landscape had expanded, and cameras and recorders were present at every campaign meeting. This provided the necessary sound bites for the political parties to utilize in their advertisement campaigns in real time. These approaches were more restrictive before the 1990s because the media landscape had not been liberalized at that time, so fewer Jamaicans had had access to mass media and were thus unable to keep abreast of national issues.

The second factor was the marked improvement in technology because of the liberalization of the media and telecommunications sectors. With the press of a button, an image could be captured via a cellular phone and the information transferred to another device in real time, courtesy of the Internet.

Finally, there was political competition. During the 2002 elections, the views of both parties converged, as they expressed similar sentiments on economic policies. At the same time, Golding had rejoined the JLP, with intimations of significant financial support from members of the private sector. So at least from the perception of voters, the party seemed united. The PNP now faced serious competition. In response, Prime Minister Patterson asked two of his senior ministers, Henry-Wilson and Robertson, to resign from the cabinet so they could manage the PNP's campaign. They were two of the most seasoned campaigners in the country and readily responded to the request.

In an interview with Robertson, he pointed out that this decision was a strategic and psychological one. There was a prevailing view within the society that no political party could win more than two terms, and yet the PNP was going for its fourth consecutive victory. The concept was having a psychological impact on PNP workers, who believed that a win was impossible. A powerful signal needed to be sent to them that the leadership was taking the election seriously and, more important, going for victory. The stage was now set for a competitive election campaign.

As noted earlier, the convergence of views between the PNP and the JLP on economic policies meant that both parties needed to find creative ways to distinguish their ideologies. The PNP's return to power in 1989 saw it abandon most of its democratic socialist policies of the 1970s, and its government required citizens to pay for education and health services. More important, it reneged on a commitment made in the 1980s to remove the special fee for tertiary students that the Seaga regime had introduced.

The JLP also recognized what was taking place within the society and sought to distinguish itself from the PNP by placing the issue of free education up to the secondary level on the campaign agenda. As pointed out earlier, this was of tremendous importance to national development and triggered intense discussion in the public sphere. It resonated among citizens and forced the PNP to go on the defensive.

It had consolidated the varied education fees through a mechanism known as "cost-sharing". But the most vulnerable still experienced difficulties paying for their children's education; consequently, Seaga's new education policy resonated strongly.

Apart from the new approach to education policy that the Patterson-led PNP was forced to communicate in the 2002 election, it was also compelled to remind voters of Seaga's history with education. A major propaganda operation was launched, and citizens were first reminded through diverse messages in the media and public speeches that Seaga had opposed Manley's free education policy of the 1970s and equated it to communism. Citizens were also reminded of the retrenchment in the education sector in the 1980s under the structural adjustment programmes implemented by the Seaga regime. Of significance was the cess introduced for tertiary students in the 1980s. These arguments discredited Seaga and the JLP and contributed to the PNP holding on for its political life in 2002. The PNP won thirty-four of the possible sixty seats. The voter turnout was 59.06 per cent (ECJ 2002).

The PNP lost sixteen of the fifty seats it had won in 1997, of which eight were in middle-class constituencies (table 3). This group placed a high premium on education, had high incomes and decent housing, and enjoyed a decent living standard.

The argument that free education was a considerable factor in the 2002 election is substantiated by supportive data from the 2007 election. In the 2007 election, Seaga was not a factor. He had retired from national politics in 2005 and was replaced by a new leader – Golding. The JLP continued to promote free education on the campaign agenda. Up to July 2007, the JLP trailed the PNP in public opinion polls such as the *Gleaner*-commissioned poll published on 1 July 2007, which indicated that 38 per cent of voters were supporting the PNP (to the JLP's 31 per cent). However, the moment the JLP intensified their campaign focus on free education was a game changer.

The dialectics of free education came to the forefront of the campaign, as the election was scheduled for early September and citizens were in the midst of preparing their children for the fall school term. The issue dominated the

Table 3. Election Outcomes by Constituencies in 1997 and 2002

Constituency	1997	2002
East Kingston	PNP	PNP
Central Kingston	PNP	PNP
West Kingston	JLP	JLP
East-Rural St Andrew	PNP	PNP
*East St Andrew	PNP	JLP
East-Central St Andrew	PNP	PNP
*North-East St Andrew	PNP	JLP
*North-Central St Andrew	JLP	JLP
*North-West St Andrew	JLP	JLP
South St Andrew	PNP	PNP
South-West St Andrew	PNP	PNP
*South-East St Andrew	PNP	PNP
West-Central St Andrew	JLP	JLP
*West-Rural St Andrew	PNP	JLP
West St Andrew	PNP	PNP
North-East St Catherine	PNP	JLP
North-West St Catherine	PNP	PNP
East-Central St Catherine	PNP	PNP
West-Central St Catherine	PNP	JLP
Central St Catherine	JLP	JLP
South-Central St Catherine	PNP	PNP
South-West St Catherine	PNP	JLP
*South-East St Catherine	PNP	PNP
*South St Catherine	PNP	PNP
North Clarendon	PNP	PNP
North-Central Clarendon	PNP	JLP
North-West Clarendon	JLP	PNP
Central Clarendon	JLP	JLP
South-West Clarendon	PNP	PNP
South-East Clarendon	PNP	JLP
North-East Manchester	JLP	JLP
North-West Manchester	PNP	PNP
*Central Manchester	PNP	PNP
South Manchester	PNP	PNP
North-East St Elizabeth	PNP	PNP
North-West St Elizabeth	JLP	JLP
*South-East St Elizabeth	PNP	PNP
South-West St Elizabeth	PNP	PNP
South-East Westmoreland	PNP	PNP
Central Westmoreland	PNP	PNP

(Continued)

Table 3. (*continued*)

Constituency	1997	2002
West Westmoreland	PNP	PNP
West Hanover	PNP	PNP
East Hanover	PNP	JLP
*North-West St James	PNP	JLP
*West-Central St James	PNP	JLP
*East-Central St James	PNP	JLP
South St James	PNP	PNP
North Trelawny	PNP	PNP
South Trelawny	PNP	JLP
*North-West St Ann	PNP	JLP
*North-East St Ann	PNP	JLP
South-East St Ann	PNP	PNP
South St Ann	PNP	JLP
Western St Mary	PNP	PNP
Central St Mary	PNP	PNP
South-East St Mary	PNP	PNP
West Portland	PNP	PNP
East Portland	PNP	PNP
East St Thomas	PNP	PNP
West St Thomas	PNP	JLP

Source: ECJ (1997, 2002).

*Constituencies with a strong middle-class population. Fifteen constituencies fit this categorization. There were eight which swung to the JLP in the 2002 election, thus giving them command over ten of these constituencies. The constituencies with a strong middle-class presence that swung to the JLP in the 2002 election were West Rural St Andrew, North-East St Andrew, East St Andrew, North-West St James, West-Central St James, East Central St James, North-West St Ann and North-East St Ann. The JLP previously had control over North-West St Andrew and North-Central St Andrew. It is clear that the PNP came under intense political pressure in the 2002 elections. Apart from the eight middle-class constituencies that were lost, there were extraordinary swings in the other constituencies in favour of the JLP as well.

campaign trail as the Golding-led JLP engaged in an aggressive advertising campaign. Their messenger was now Golding, and the PNP had no basis to discredit him on the issue of free education. Moreover, the PNP had not honoured the commitment that they had made in the 2002 election to phase out the cost-sharing policy, which brought their credibility into question.

The JLP secured thirty-two of the sixty seats in the 2007 elections, which at that time was the narrowest margin since the nation achieved political independence in 1962. This included another constituency with a large middle-class

Table 4. Election Outcomes by Constituencies Heavily Populated with Middle-Class Voters in the 2007 Election

Constituencies	2002	Margin	2007	Margin
West Rural St Andrew	6,640/8,406 (JLP)	1,766	9,578/7,257 (JLP)	2,321
North-Central St Andrew	3,425/5,831 (JLP)	2,406	3,488/6,254 (JLP)	2,766
North-West St Andrew	3,708/5,480 (JLP)	1,772	3,909/5,794 (JLP)	1,885
North-East St Andrew	2,811/6,033 (JLP)	3,222	5,764/2,814 (JLP)	2,950
East St Andrew	5,556/5,642 (JLP)	96	5,907/5,308 (JLP)	599
South-East St Andrew	4,959/4,103 (PNP)	856	4,618/5,187 (PNP)	569
South-East St Catherine	6,805/5,443 (PNP)	1,362	7,292/6,987 (PNP)	305
South St Catherine	8,513/6,980 (PNP)	1,533	9,337/7,917 (PNP)	1,420
Central Manchester	8,307/7,185 (PNP)	1,122	8,453/8,338 (PNP)	115
South-East St Elizabeth	7,507/7,425 (PNP)	82	8,520/9,064 (JLP)	544
North-West St James	7,004/9,654 (JLP)	2,650	7,482/5,569 (JLP)	1,913
West-Central St James	5,980/7,098 (JLP)	1,118	7,752/7,216 (JLP)	536
East-Central St James	5,170/6,394 (JLP)	1,224	8,398/6,637 (JLP)	1,762
North-West St Ann	7,362/7,564 (JLP)	202	8,210/7,346 (JLP)	864
North-East St Ann	9,981/11,155 (JLP)	1,174	11,632/9,610 (JLP)	2,022

Source: ECJ (2002, 2007).

population in South-East St Elizabeth. The JLP secured 49.98 per cent of the votes, to the PNP's 49.35 per cent (ECJ 2007). Trends signalled significantly reduced margins for the PNP in other constituencies with large middle-class populations (table 4). As a consequence of the 2007 election, the JLP took control of eleven of the fifteen middle-class constituencies.

The data presented in this chapter makes it clear that Jamaica has seen an evolution in political campaigning over the past forty years. It has moved from mundane street meetings to more sophisticated media campaigns. The political parties have developed different approaches towards campaigning and communicating their messages to Jamaican citizens. Up to the 1997 election, the Seaga-led JLP maintained a conservative approach to political campaigning, with a heavy focus on street meetings and house-to-house visits. The reasons for this approach are made clear in an article by Seaga (2007, G1) in the *Gleaner*: "Jamaica is not a literary society; it is an oral one, passing on information by the spoken word. The spoken word is transmitted in speech and news items through radio and television. But it is the political platform that serves as the best means of communication to the general public."

Seaga (2007, G3) further argued: "This presents a problem. Language has to be tailored to the level of understanding of the people. This means using catch phrases, buzzwords and street language. Automatically, this determines what type of subjects can be addressed. It rules out complex arguments on issues, unless the arguments are down to their simplest common denominators."

The approach by the Seaga-led JLP contributed to their defeat in four national elections since 1980. During this time, the JLP won only two elections, including the snap election of 1983, which was uncontested. It must be noted that when the party won the 1980 elections, they adopted a more pragmatic approach towards political campaigning, utilizing a mixture of traditional and modern means that included radio and television advertisements, newspaper advertisements, campaign songs, community meetings and mass rallies. Seaga's statement also indicated that the JLP underestimated the intelligence of Jamaican citizens. It is true that messages must be tailored to the audience; however, it is also imprudent to misjudge the audience's intellectual capacity.

Conversely, during the period under study, the Manley- and Patterson-led PNP adopted a more pragmatic approach to political campaigning. They utilized all the possible approaches to campaigning, implementing a mixture of conventional and modern techniques. This approach undoubtedly contributed to the party's victories.

Having examined the campaign approaches of both political parties in Jamaica since 1972 through documentary evidence, five fundamental factors have been identified for consideration by political communication specialists in the Caribbean. These are personality, fearmongering in election campaigning, culture, language and race.

Personality

The factor of personality has played a prominent role in the Jamaican political landscape ever since the country gained adult suffrage in 1944. Dominant figures such as Norman Manley and Alexander Bustamante were constant staples within the body politic of the society. Citizens could be seen and heard imitating these two leaders during that era. The matter took on renewed significance during the 1970s, however, when both Manley and Seaga became leaders of their political organizations. Manley was very charismatic, while Seaga was more autocratic but had a compelling personality. Patterson was calm and technocratic but very strategic in his thinking and action.

During the era of leadership by Manley, Seaga and Patterson, the media, especially television, became a major source of information dissemination. Citizens could see these politicians' faces and hear their voices, so they could now identify them. They became household names in Jamaica, and wherever they went, as leaders, they attracted significant public attention. Therefore, the personalities of these leaders played a prominent role in their communication strategies and helped to mobilize support for their administrations.

Fearmongering

Fear has figured prominently in Jamaica's modern political history. This occurs in situations where political parties use a particular message to scare voters, with the desired effect being refusal to vote for the opponent. Oftentimes the message is false, but if it is repeated enough, then it becomes a truism.

In the period under study, we saw that fearmongering was prominent in the 1980 elections. The Seaga-led JLP presented the argument to Jamaican citizens that if the Manley-led PNP won, it would introduce communism. This argument was based on Manley's close association with communist states such as the USSR and Cuba. Seaga knew from his study of Jamaican culture that Jamaicans placed an intrinsic value on their freedom. Therefore, he played on their perception that the introduction of communism in the island would violate and dismantle that freedom. The message was produced and constantly repeated in advertisements and political speeches and contributed to the defeat of the PNP in 1980. This has been an effective communication strategy used by JLP leaders to mobilize support for their party. First used in the referendum of 1961 by Alexander Bustamante, it was repeated by Seaga in 1980 and served as the core of his communication strategy.

Culture

Culture – the values, norms, practices and attitudes that exist within a society – has also played a dominant role in Jamaican political campaigning. For example, there is a deep love for reggae and food, both of which form part of daily Jamaican life. Reggae, the dominant form of music, can be heard in every sector of the society, while there is a proliferation of food festivals across the island.

Politicians and political parties have recognized this critical nature of culture in mass mobilization and citizen participation and have sought to exploit it over the years. Political rallies, street meetings and party conferences have all featured reggae music and artists as part of their agenda. Any amount of food and liquor can be had at these functions, as the political parties go to extremes to attract voters.

Prior to 1972, folk songs could be heard at various political meetings across the island. In the 1972 election, the Manley-led PNP rode a wave of popular songs that were being played at dances and on the radio. The adoption of these songs by the Manley-led PNP contributed to the party's victory in 1972.

Based on the experience of 1972 and the growth of reggae in Jamaica, the PNP for the first time in 1976 introduced a specific campaign song, linked to the reggae rhythm. In this song ("The Message"), the lyrics were specifically linked to the programmes and policies that were implemented by the Manley regime between 1972 and 1976. The song proved to be a winner; it is still regarded by members and supporters of the PNP as one of their favourite political songs, eliciting enthusiastic responses when it is played at any of their political rallies or street meetings. Its introduction in 1976 paved the way for the use of campaign songs in all subsequent elections by both political parties, as this has proved to be an effective way of communicating programmes and policies. This means of communication can be seen as a conflation of the production and circulation phase of the model of Hall and colleagues and McLuhan's theory of the medium being the message. It captures the production and the medium for distributing political messages instantaneously. All the leaders evaluated here have used this strategy to communicate their programmes and policies during the periods reviewed in this chapter.

Language

Language – the way that humans communicate with an audience orally, through signing or in print – plays a critical role in any political campaign. Generally, the politician who is best able to use the language of the people is the one who is most effective in winning the support of the voters. In 1972, Michael Manley was able to capture the minds and hearts of citizens with the slogans "Hail di man" and "Power to the People". These words conveyed a notion of sincerity to citizens and gave them the feeling that they were really in charge. This was also within the context of citizens' experience with the Shearer administration, with which there had been conflict, and some had felt that their powers were severely restricted.

In the 1980 elections, the buzzwords for the JLP were *deliverance* and *freedom*. Again, their use evoked the PNP's flirtation with communist regimes and the perception that Manley was about to introduce communism on the island. The JLP projected itself as the party that would free citizens from "political and economic bondage" and make "dunnie [money] jingle in pocket[s]". The theme resonated with the electorate and contributed to the largest victory of the JLP in any election to date.

In the 1989 election, the PNP used a simple but effective set of words to form the base of their campaign. These were "We Put People First", which connected to the perception that Seaga and the JLP were uncaring. Social services were experiencing major cuts due to the policy prescriptions of multilateral institutions, and Seaga and the JLP were blamed for this. Consequently, Jamaicans viewed the administration as uncaring and voted against them.

In the 2002 election, the PNP used another set of words that resonated with the voters. Recognizing the advances made with technology across the island, the PNP used the slogan "Log On to Progress". The organization capitalized on the computer revolution taking place in the country and used it to its advantage. Citizens identified with the message and gave the PNP its fourth consecutive term in office.

The political actors on both sides recognized the issues confronting the people and adapted their own ordinary language to communicate with them. In the production of their messages, the language is given prominence, making it easier for citizens to understand what is being communicated. The political party that gives utility to such an approach will enjoy political success.

Race

The final factor that figured prominently in political campaigning in Jamaica was race – the phenotypical image that distinguishes one individual from another. Jamaica has a predominantly black population (95 per cent). However, between the time when the country gained universal adult suffrage in 1944 and 1992, the country had been governed by white leaders, with the exception of the Shearer administration (1967–1972). The ascension of Patterson as prime minister of Jamaica began a trend of black leaders at the helm. It is instructive to note that Patterson, a black man, is the longest-serving prime minister of Jamaica (fourteen years), as well as the only one to have been voted in for three consecutive terms. Of the six prime ministers up to 2002, four were white Jamaicans and the other two were black. Stone (1973) acknowledged the fact that race plays a pivotal role in the political process of Jamaica.

On the campaign trail, individuals would make reference to Patterson's race. On one occasion Patterson was reported saying, "If I should come into the crowd, it would be difficult for you to distinguish between me and you." These statements would solicit tremendous response from the audience, as it was construed as a personal contrast between Patterson and his rival, Seaga, a white Jamaican.

In the 1993 election campaign, as discussed previously, Seaga made the mistake of referring to Patterson as a "black scandal-bag". This reference was construed as a racial attack and caused considerable disquiet in the society. The statement figured prominently in advertisements by the PNP across the media and contributed to the victory of that political party in the election. Those who have responsibility for developing political messages for leaders and their political parties must be sensitive to issues regarding race, as it is important in order to design messages that communicate and connect with citizens.

From the evidence presented in this chapter, it can be concluded that Patterson is the leader who has been most effective in communicating his programmes and policies to citizens. He has managed to integrate all five of these factors in his communication strategies and used them successfully to mobilize citizens to participate in the political process, thus securing victories at the polls.

8.

New Media, Political Communication and Citizen Participation in Jamaica

Since the 1990s, there has been a radical transformation of the global media landscape (Dahlgren 2000b). The advancement of modern technologies has metamorphosed the media environment, allowing an increasing number of ordinary citizens to gain access to the media and their leaders (Blumler and Kavanagh 1999). The advent of the Internet facilitated the development of Facebook, YouTube, Twitter, texting and other forms of instant communication. This brought about a new and different media landscape. In this new environment, citizens are more demanding in their claims that their rights must be protected by their government, as well as for greater accountability and transparency from their leaders. This chapter highlights and describes the new media environment, how it was developed, what it entails and how it has contributed to what I regard as the fourth wave of democracy currently sweeping the globe.

In the early 1960s, scholars and researchers were engrossed in developing ways of transmitting information in a faster, more efficient manner. The result was increased use of the computer, satellite and telephone, which over time evolved into the development of the Internet (Cerf and Kahn 1974).

Ever since the collapse of communism, there has been an extensive transformation in the global media landscape. This is largely due to the introduction of modern technologies such as cellular phones and the Internet as a means of communicating across the globe. According to the Federal Networking Council (1995, para. 5):

> "Internet" refers to the global information system that – (i) is logically linked together by a globally unique address space based on the Internet Protocol (IP) or its subsequent extensions/follow-ons; (ii) is able to support communications using the Transmission Control Protocol/Internet Protocol (TCP/IP) suite or its subsequent extensions/follow ons, and/or other IP-compatible protocols; and (iii) provides, uses or makes accessible, either publicly or privately, high-level services layered on the communications and related infrastructure described herein.

In its burgeoning stage, the technology was used primarily for research in medicine, the military, and the academic and the business spheres. Access to this innovation was by and large confined to a few individuals who were involved in research. However, as time evolved, the birth of a new economic global order, along with the collapse of communism, propelled the rise of the Internet as a means of transmitting information to the general public.

Computers and the advancement of telephones were a vital part of the new economic order, which provided a perfect environment for the Internet to thrive and develop. Ultimately, it became the catalyst which linked trade, politics, sports, culture, science, education and every other facet of life in the world (Giddens 1991).

This new media was very interactive, allowing individuals to communicate through the use of the Internet and cellular technology. Podcasts, Facebook, Twitter, blogging, e-mail and other platforms were all features of the new means of communication. It was instant, unregulated and, more important, it extended to individuals in remote parts of the globe (Dahlgren 2005). The new media basically revolutionizes how citizens communicate with each other (Forbes 2012), and this has profound implications for political communication. Accordingly, it is important to contextualize the applicability of the Internet in political communication.

What do some of these new media entail? How were they developed? *Podcast* is a relatively new term that replaces the word *webcast,* which was a dominant part of the digital genre in the early days of the Internet, especially since the development of the iPod (Hamersley 2004). A podcast (or nonstreamed webcast) is a series of digital media files (either audio or video) that are released episodically and often downloaded through web syndication. Simply put, a podcast is generally a delayed digitalized broadcast available on the Internet for viewing at an individual's convenience.

Facebook is one of the novel inventions of the Internet in the twenty-first century. Developed by Mark Zuckerberg in February 2004, the social networking website was established to link individuals across the world. Since its inception, it has received an average of four hundred million visits per month. Citizens across the globe have been utilizing the website for diverse purposes, one of which is to promote and support democracy. According to an article published on the ACE Forum (Novendstern 2011, para. 7):

> It's not crazy to claim, then, that democracies and information networks are in some fundamental way aligned in their structure and logic: free individuals (nodes in a network) share information freely with other people (distribute information across the network) in public places like town centres, libraries, the post office, the National Mall and the printing press (the public information platforms that make democracy work). In the process, they give substance to the idea of a sovereign – they create "a people" with a "will".

Facebook and Twitter are nothing more (and nothing less) than new tools for this older, democratic function – the distribution of information across networks, communicative actions among citizens, the creating of shared meaning (Novendstern 2011). At the time, Novendstern was participating in a discussion on events taking place in Egypt and its quest for democracy. The use of Facebook was a prominent source of accessing and disseminating information to the Egyptians as they pressed for greater political and economic freedom. The role of the social media network was so powerful in the Egyptian uprising (part of the so-called Arab Spring) that the government made several attempts to disrupt connectivity. This prompted appeals from President Barack Obama and Secretary of State Hillary Clinton of the United States to the Egyptian authorities not to meddle with the rights of citizens to freedom of expression and information (Obama 2012).

The use of Facebook in the transformation of democracies and the reformation of autocratic regimes across the world has been hailed by President Obama as a novel American innovation (Obama 2012). In his State of the Union address in 2012, the president cited social media, particularly Facebook, as a necessary element of the universal right to the freedom of expression and access to information (Obama 2012). The transformative effect of Facebook is evident in the shaping of democracy in the modern political context.

Twitter is another form of new media that has affected modern democracy. It was created in March 2006 by Jack Dorsey as a means of sending short, instant messages to followers. It is estimated that Twitter has over three hundred million active users a month, with approximately one hundred million active users a day.

Twitter is a social networking and microblogging website which allows its users to send and receive messages called *tweets* – text-based posts comprising up to 280 characters highlighted on a user's profile page. Individuals have been using this new means of communication to promote a wide range of products and causes. Progressive politicians in democracies across the world have been using Twitter as a means of keeping in close contact with their constituents. This was one of the means by which President Obama stayed in touch with his supporters in the 2008 and 2012 elections and was able to mobilize a large cadre of young people.

YouTube is another media phenomenon that has been affecting the development of democracy across the world. It was developed by Chad Hurley, Steve Chen and Jawed Karim in February 2005. YouTube is a video-sharing website that provides both amateur and professional videos to clients across the world. Indeed, the invention of YouTube has triggered a novelty on the Internet: Individuals can watch videos of what is taking place across the globe from their computers or cellular phones. Similarly, they can use a digital video recorder or a simple cellular phone, to upload video recordings from their communities onto the YouTube website.

This is how the world has been able to witness some of the uprisings and protests for greater democracy across the world. In 2009, for example, the world witnessed the death of a prodemocracy advocate, Neda Agha-Soltan, in Iran. The video of Agha-Soltan dying, in full view of the world, went on to win the Polk Award, one of the most prestigious journalism awards (Trussel 2010). It is clear that over the past twenty years, the world has witnessed a revolution in the media landscape, and this has profound implications for democracy. Jenkins and Thorburn (2003, 12) noted:

> But in 2003, if we ask whether the revolution will be digitized, the answer is "Yes". The Web's low barriers to entry ensure greater access than ever before to innovative, even revolutionary ideas. Those silenced by corporate media have been among the first, as Pool predicted, to transform their computers into printing presses. This access to the World Wide Web has empowered revolutionaries, reactionaries and racists alike. It has also engendered fear in the gatekeeper intermediaries and their allies. One person's diversity, no doubt, is another person's anarchy.

The Internet opened up a whole new world of possibilities for citizens worldwide. People can now communicate and trade with each other in a manner that was unfathomable fifty years ago. Since its launch, the multipurpose Internet has enabled the expansion of political dialogue among citizens worldwide. Citizens have been able to retrieve information and to participate in active discussions on many issues in this public sphere (Dahlgren 2002). Habermas's (1989, 52) arguments on the public sphere led to an interesting observation:

> With the rise of a sphere of the social, over whose regulation public opinion battled with public power, the theme of the modern (in contrast to the ancient) public sphere shifted from the properly political tasks of a citizenry acting in common (i.e., administration of law as regards internal affairs and military survival as regards external affairs) to the more properly civic tasks of a society engaged in critical public debate (i.e., the protection of a commercial economy). The political task of the bourgeois public sphere was the regulation of civil society (in contradistinction to the res publica). With the background experience of a private sphere that had become interiorized human closeness it challenged the established authority of the monarch; in this sense its character was from the beginning both private and polemical at once.

According to Dahlgren (2005, 148):

> In schematic terms, a functioning public sphere is understood as a constellation of communicative spaces in society that permit the circulation of information, ideas, and debates ideally in an unfettered manner and also the formation of political will

(i.e., public opinion). These spaces, in which the mass media and now, more recently, the newer interactive media figure prominently, also serve to facilitate communicative links between citizens and the power holders of society.

Dahlgren's definition drew on arguments from Habermas. Implicit in the arguments from both of them is that the ability to access computers enables citizens to freely participate in any dialogue on the Internet. This participation, as can be seen, has exploded since the 1990s. Estimates suggest that over two billion citizens have access to these online conversations. This is approximately 30 per cent of the world's population, and it is expected to accelerate over the next ten years as the telecommunications industry across the globe becomes more liberalized.

Dahlgren (2005, 148) further postulated:

> For about a decade now, many researchers and other observers have been asking whether the Internet will have or is already having an impact on the public sphere and, if so, the attributes of this impact. Such discussions become unavoidably framed by the general international consensus, emerging since the early 1990s that democracy has hit upon hard times; more specifically, the hope is often expressed that the Internet will somehow have a positive impact on democracy and help to alleviate its ills.

The Internet has over the past twenty years contributed significantly to the expansion and improvement of democracy across the world. This is greatly manifested in the number of countries which have subscribed to democratic tendencies since 1989. In East Europe, Asia, Africa and Latin America, many countries have moved from being totalitarian regimes to democracy. This is largely attributed to the efforts to liberalize global economies, and the Internet has facilitated this process towards democracy.

But what exactly is this concept of democracy? In its classical sense, Abraham Lincoln characterized democracy as "government of the people, by the people and for the people". This classical notion of democracy has not been experienced in modern times. As a matter of fact, scholars such as Robert Dahl (1971) reject this notion of democracy in the modern context, regards what exists as polyarchy and in this context, refers to it as "a continuing responsiveness of government to the preferences of its citizens considered as political equals" (1).

Dahl further postulated that for this brand of democracy to exist, there must be economic development, equality, subcultural cleavages, foreign control and the beliefs of political activists. Dahl's work set the stage for further elucidation of the subject of democracy. It makes it easier for scholars to operationalize the concept. The term *economic development* can be divided into two segments – socioeconomic order and the levels of competition in that socioeconomic order. This is largely because economic development encapsulates more than a mere calculation of the gross domestic product. It also constitutes the improvement of the social, economic, physical and environmental infrastructure of the society, which will automatically lead to the improvement of the standard of living of the people within that society.

Equality refers to a situation where individuals within a society have the same opportunity to participate and progress, regardless of race, class or religious group. This opportunity to participate and develop must include basic civil liberties such as freedom of choice, freedom of expression, freedom of association, the right to vote and the right to defend oneself under the law, all of which characterize a just and equitable society.

Subcultural cleavage is an important variable in the concept of democracy. This is because these subgroupings can either make or break the democratic process through insurrections, civil war, coups and other such destabilizing factors. Thus, subcultural cleavages refer to the different subgroupings along class, racial or religious lines, having ideas or interests which are inconsistent with those of the larger group in the society or the rest of the society as a whole (Dahl 1971). In Jamaica, for example, there is ample evidence of class cleavage.

Some development theorists believe that the level of foreign control has a major influence on democracy. This is because of the fact that these individuals possess well-needed capital for investment and growth. *Foreign control,* therefore, refers to the amount of foreign capital in an economy and the leverage that foreign countries and organizations possess, which may allow them to dictate the level of development within that economy. This can be dangerous for any economy – not to mention society in general – as the holders of foreign capital can withdraw at any time.

A *political activist* is an individual who is involved in the political process on a day-to-day basis. The term includes the party leaders and officials, and even area leaders found in communities. These individuals, according to Dahl, will defend the democratic process because of their belief in it. This is why we have been seeing more and more political activists on the Internet, using Facebook, Twitter and YouTube to advocate their causes, due to the wave of economic liberalization which swept the globe during the 1990s and opened up economies to competition in the marketplace.

Through the liberalization of the telecommunications industry, the Internet has become more accessible to citizens across the globe and has provided a rich opportunity for them to discuss political matters in the public sphere. The public sphere has three constitutive dimensions: structures, representation and interaction. Dahlgren (2005, 149) describes these as follows: "The structural dimension has to do with the formal institutional features. This includes media organisations, their political economy, ownership, control, regulation and issues of their financing, as well as the legal frameworks defining the freedoms of and constraints on communication."

These three dimensions provide an analytical starting point for examining the public sphere of any given society or for analysing the contribution of any communication technology. In this context, it would be pertinent to examine the Jamaican experience since the advent of new media, in order to assess its impact on the public sphere and on democracy. Prior to engaging in such discussion, it would be wise to examine the fourth wave of democracy gathering momentum worldwide.

Huntington (1991) published a seminal academic work entitled *The Third Wave: Democratization in the Late Twentieth Century*, in which he argued that the new wave of democracy in the twentieth century had its genesis in the Portugal Revolution of 1974. He argued that this was accelerated with assistance from the Helsinki Final Act of 1975 and the change in US foreign policy from support for regimes loyal to the West to an emphasis on civil and political rights. Huntington suggested that this contributed to over sixty countries in Africa, Eastern Europe, Asia and Latin America, adapting to democratic tendencies.

What is conspicuously absent from Huntington's list of contributing factors in this rush to democracy was the prominent use of the media and modern technology. The pervasiveness of the Internet and other forms of new media were absent at the time of this wave. But traditional media certainly was present and played a pivotal role in the transformation and expansion of worldwide democracy.

Huntington (1991) noted that this third wave of democracy went through the following processes:

- Transformation – A top-down (elite-controlled) change from within government (as postulated by theoreticians of the modernization theory some thirty years earlier)
- Transplacement – A negotiated reform of regime and government
- Replacement – Regime breakdown (rupture) and the collapse of authoritarianism

Fast forward into the twenty-first century – there are glaring similarities with the emerging fourth wave of democracy. The genesis this time stems from the invasion of Iraq by US and allied forces in 2003. The incursion resulted in the toppling of the Saddam Hussein regime and saw the establishment of a multiethnic administration which represented the different tribes in Iraq. Since then, Iraq has had two elections where citizens democratically elect their own government.

The events in Iraq have had ripple effects in the Middle East and parts of Africa as citizens began to vocalize their demands for a change in the process of governance and democracy. Tunisia, Egypt, Libya and other countries in North Africa with autocratic regimes have all been experiencing mass protests and demonstrations. Up to the present day, no one can accurately predict where this fourth wave is heading and where it will end.

Processes identical to those noted by Huntington are recurring. Transformation, transplacement and replacement have all been incorporated into this fourth wave. Thus far, with the aid of new media, citizens have rebelled against their governments, intensifying their demands for greater transparency and accountability and advocating for a greater stake in the economic bases of their societies.

At some point in the milieu, the elites joined the protest. However, they emerged at a point when the protests were far advanced and then hijacked it. In Egypt and Tunisia, a strong and assertive citizen movement, assisted by modern technologies and new media, resulted in a radical transformation in the government apparatus. The regimes which had control for decades had to succumb to the demands of the people.

I have sought to analyse the effectiveness of governmental communication on citizens of Jamaica, with particular focus on the period 1972–2006. This era enveloped the leadership of Michael Manley, Seaga and Patterson as heads of the Jamaican government. During this period, traditional media was the dominant means of communicating with citizens. As a matter of fact, new media did not become a part of the political landscape until the 2002 elections. Even then, it was never a major feature because the telecommunication industry had been liberalized only recently.

In 2002, websites were introduced by the two major political parties, which provided voters with information on candidates and manifestos. By the time Jamaica reached the 2007 elections, a major transformation had taken place through the use of new media by the political parties. Facebook, blogs, Twitter, text messaging and chat rooms have since become a standard feature of the political campaign. For example, in the 2007 national elections, the political parties sent several mass text messages to registered voters in constituencies across the island. This was made possible because by then, nearly two million Jamaicans had access to cellular phones (STATIN 2008). Simultaneously, a number of party officials could be seen and heard in chat rooms, espousing the various achievements and policies of their political parties.

Media websites contain links to Facebook and Twitter. Thousands of Jamaicans have since logged on to both sites, and they have contributed to the dialectics taking place in the public sphere. For example, the public enquiry of the

Manatt, Phelps and Phillips affair in 2010 saw many Jamaicans expressing their opinions during the deliberations in social media. Manatt, Phelps and Phillips, a law firm based in the United States, was hired by the government of Jamaica to lobby the United States for the extradition of a JLP supporter and a don in West Kingston named Christopher "Dudus" Coke. This engagement led to a public enquiry into the matter. The opinions of citizens could be seen on the websites of the two major newspapers, the *Gleaner* and the *Jamaica Observer*.

As time passed, more and more Jamaicans have become attached to new media. The liberalization of the telecommunications industry which took place early in the twenty-first century contributed to more and more citizens having access to Facebook, Twitter and YouTube. The operators of telephone services in the country have all recorded tremendous sales in varied devices which allow instant messaging to take place. One of the main cellular providers, Digicel, indicated that it had over seventy thousand subscribers to Blackberry, a service that enables a customer to engage in a wide range of Internet-related activities, such as Facebook, Twitter, YouTube and instant messaging.

A survey conducted in 2011 by a team led by Hopeton Dunn of the University of the West Indies revealed that approximately 94 per cent of Jamaicans had access to cellular phones, 24 per cent of Jamaicans had a computer and approximately 16 per cent had Internet access in their homes. The situation is more encouraging, though, as it examines individuals as opposed to households, as 42 per cent of individuals indicate access to the Internet either at home or elsewhere.

The low levels of access to the Internet and ownership of computers by Jamaicans are largely attributed to the issue of cost. Therefore, it means that policymakers have to implement programmes and policies which will contribute to greater access to the Internet and ownership of computers by Jamaicans, which in turn will result in citizens enjoying more of the offerings of new media and the global economic environment. This is even more important for vulnerable groups, such as people with disabilities. Dunn's study showed that less than 1 per cent of the respondents with a disability had access to the Internet.

To facilitate access and citizens' integration with technology, several initiatives are required. Some of these include the following:

- Removal of all duties and taxes on computers, which will result in a significant cost reduction.
- Provision of further improvements to the regulatory environment, which will lead to greater broadband access to the Internet.
- Expediting the installation of computers and Internet services in all government-operated schools across the island by removing all

bureaucratic impediments to the Universal Access Fund, which was established to provide greater access of the Internet to Jamaicans.

• Making Wi-Fi available to all major town centres across the country so that citizens can easily access the Internet. If these policy and programmatic initiatives are not executed in the near future, only the elites of the society will be able to take advantage of the offerings of new media and the global economic landscape.

Notwithstanding the low levels of access to the Internet by households in Jamaica, the country has seen the government expand its use of new media since 2002 to transmit information to citizens, as well as to communicate about policies and programming. Through the diverse ministries, websites have been established to provide information to and solicit data from citizens. The JIS has its own website, which provides critical information to the public. Parliament has now established its own website, and citizens can access important information on legislation that it passes.

It is clear that there has been a significant transformation in the media landscape in Jamaica. More citizens have access to telephones, and this allows them greater access to the Internet and increased capacity for accessing social networking sites to participate in discourses relating to societal issues. They no longer depend on groups or branches to disseminate information relating to politics in their communities.

Furthermore, all the traditional media companies in Jamaica offer new media options which allow their clients to keep in constant contact. At the governmental level, the ministries and agencies have been adopting a similar approach, making serious attempts to stay in touch with citizens. These options and services were unavailable to policymakers prior to 2002. The ability of governments in Jamaica to respond continuously to the needs of its citizens, through effective communication, has now been greatly enhanced. The question of whether this availability is helping to improve governance and democracy remains to be seen.

Very little research, if any, has been done on this area of Jamaican political life. Therefore, it is impossible to state definitively the extent of the effect of new media on the quality of democracy in the country. The state of democracy is of major concern, as citizens have been avoiding the political process. More than 40 per cent of the population expressed dissatisfaction with the nature of democracy in the country during the 1990s, but to date, Jamaica has not experienced the sort of mass protest that has taken place in the Middle East. Is it that citizens have found new means of expressing and ventilating their dissatisfactions through new media? Dunn (2012) pointed to the dominant use of the Internet in Jamaica by citizens below the age of 34. Interestingly, this is the majority of the approximately 40 per cent of Jamaicans who are frustrated with the political process (Anderson 2015).

To summarize, the dialectics about the poor health of democracy in Jamaica and the globe intensified during the 1990s, at about the same time that the Internet was rapidly leading a media revolution. Scholars and observers optimistically connected the two phenomena. The proliferation of the media, especially the Internet, would assist in remedying the challenges confronting democracies across the globe (Anderson and Cornfield 2003). The Internet has made it possible for individuals to communicate more effectively with each other through the proliferation of social media such as Twitter, Facebook and YouTube. Information on virtually every sphere of life is readily available and accessible through these sources. Governments, including that of Jamaica, have become part of this development and have been establishing a plethora of social media facilities to communicate with their citizens. They realize that if they are to curtail the growing tide of citizen apathy and frustration with the political process, new media must play a leading role. There has been an intensification of the effort of leaders and their administrations to communicate with citizens in Jamaica via new media. However, no one can definitively state the extent to which this has contributed to an improvement or decline in democracy in the country. The situation demonstrates a gap in the phenomena and grounds for further research.

9.

Closing Analysis of Findings
and Recommendations

Since Jamaica gained political independence in 1962, the country has had to confront a number of challenges. One of these is the growing voter apathy among Jamaican citizens. As the country matured, a decline in the level of participation of citizens in the political process became evident. This has been manifested by significantly lower voter turnout for elections since the early 1990s. In the early stages of Jamaica's democracy, voter participation hovered around 85 per cent, but this declined significantly to less than 55 per cent in the 2011 election.

Multiple arguments have been posited for this decrease, but no specific work has been done to determine the extent to which the communication of programmes and policies of leaders and their political organizations has been effective in stimulating the interest of the masses. Acknowledging the epistemological political communications deficit, this book was written to provide answers to some of the questions that have contributed to the level of apathy towards democracy in Jamaica. In particular, it has scrutinized the communication strategies used by leaders and their administrations to inform citizens of programmes and policies.

The main aim of the book was to analyse mediated political communication in modern Jamaica during the period from 1972 to 2006 by determining how communication strategies of selected political leaders have served to engage citizen participation of the Jamaican people during the period; the nature of the relationship between political leaders and citizens in mass mobilization in Jamaica; and the effects of the media representation of political masses on group membership and political party involvement in Jamaica

I have explored the argument that "the success or failure of a leader and his political organization in modern Jamaica is closely linked to the effective communication strategy for programmes and policies". As a part of my strategy to corroborate this statement, I have relied on Hahn's (2003) arguments on freedom and order, Habermas's (1989) theory on communicative action and the public sphere, Dahl's (1971) prerequisites for democracy, Stone's (1980) theories on patron-client relationships and Lasswell's (1948) on communication, the communication models of McLuhan (1964) – the medium is the message – and the encoder/decoder theory of Hall et al. (1973). The cross-disciplinary approach served to guide the process, and my major findings are presented here.

In examining some of the foundational theoretical and conceptual arguments behind the subject of political communication, this book has shown that it is part of the process of facilitating ongoing dialogue on some fundamental issues relating to the process of decision-making. Critical to this is the "freedom versus order" debate. The dialectic on these two indispensable issues has affected on basically all major theories and practices relating to the matter.

The practice of political communication has been influenced by certain theoretical and philosophical issues ranging from liberalism to globalization. It has required an open environment in which quintessential tenets are active competition, as well as the recognition of certain fundamental individual freedoms, such as freedom of expression.

Over the years, political communication has developed out of societies that have endorsed the philosophy of liberalism. In this regard, the United States and most European countries have been practising liberal democracy and have institutionalized political communication.

Moves towards the establishment of a globalized world have also served to enhance the practice. The establishment of institutions such as the IMF, World Bank and GATT signalled the commencement of a new global order in the 1940s, which led to the promotion of the market as the primary institution for the production of goods and services. Consequently, capitalism has emerged as a dominant force in this new global order. Countries have been forced to liberalize their markets, to privatize industries that were under government control and to make way for private ownership. This has opened the door for multinational corporations to extend their tentacles into new markets, thus contributing to the transformation of values, practices and norms in developing countries. One such industry to be affected by this process is the media.

The introduction of economic liberalization, coupled with the development of modern technologies, has resulted in an explosion in the global media environment. The growth of television, the Internet and cellular phones have all contributed to media's role as the primary institution of socialization in societies that practise liberal democracy. Consequently, the practice of political communication has been enhanced as more and more societies seek to adopt this exciting approach to renewing democracy.

The growth of the media has also contributed to the development of modern political strategies to attract voters. Political propaganda, advertisements, public relations and public opinion polls are some of the approaches that have been adopted to win the hearts and minds of the public. As a result, extensive academic work has been done internationally, which has led to theories and concepts that can analyse and predict the outcome of political events.

This volume confirms that political communication best thrives in an open society where there is a free market and where the basic civil liberties are observed, with the practice thus dominant in countries such as the United States, Canada and Europe. While all the theories and concepts point to this conclusion, what we have *not* seen is the extent to which these practices have been adopted by other societies, such as those in the Caribbean, where very limited work has been done to determine the lessons of mediated political communication.

Using Jamaica as the point of departure, an analysis of this practice was conducted through an examination of the work of Michael Manley, Seaga and Patterson. Substantial focus was placed on the concepts of freedom and order in the context of modern political communication debates. However, there must be a lucid understanding of the political culture of the country if its leaders are to communicate effectively with its citizens.

We have seen that since 1962, Jamaica has been experiencing an evolution in its political culture. In the embryonic stages of its development, the family, church, trade unions and political parties were the major institutions through which values, norms and social practices were developed. These attitudes, values and practices coincided with the early phase of political communication in democracy. The family, for example, would be the institution to which the younger generation would look for influence and to determine which political organization to support. It is at the level of the family that this political dialogue on freedom and order is introduced and individuals choose a particular polit-ical ideology (that is, liberal or conservative).

Simultaneously, the political parties had pride of place in the lives of Jamai-cans, as they were a major source of information dissemination and for the garnering of scarce resources. The founders of the political parties deliberately established mechanisms to transmit and receive information on programmes and policies that they pursued or wished to pursue in the country. The groups and branches were thus the basic mechanism used by the JLP and PNP to communicate with citizens. Both parties have been enmeshed in the political dialectics on freedom and order, with the PNP adopting a more liberal perspec-tive (freedom) and the JLP a more conservative outlook (order).

Since 1992, however, we have seen a changing political culture within Jamaican society. While the family and political parties are still regarded as primordial institutions of socialization, the media has emerged as a parallel institution of notable significance. The growth of modern technologies, coupled with an aggressive economic liberalization and privatization programme, has contributed to an exponential expansion of the media landscape in Jamaica. This has contributed to citizens shifting their loyalty and respect from certain authority figures such as politicians to the hosts of talk shows.

The changes that are taking place in the political culture of Jamaica must also be seen within the context of a broader global perspective. Other exogenous factors such as the collapse of communism and the rapid move towards a globalized world have forced societies to change the way they think and their attitudes towards development. There has been homogenization of media systems throughout the world, and in this context, the media has been required to play a crucial role in linking different cultures, leading to a shift in certain traditional values and attitudes. The media, therefore, must be seen as a fundamental institution in any political communication study as it serves to shape the values, norms, personalities and attitudes within a society. Jamaica is no exception to this, and policymakers must be cognizant of these changes when designing programmes and policies for citizens.

Five issues have been made distinctly clear:

- Understanding the political culture of a society is a necessary ingredient for effective communication. There is a clear and distinct political culture emanating from social institutions such as schools, churches, trade unions, political parties and the media within Jamaica, which has been instrumental in the practice of political communication on the island. Political strategists and policymakers must understand this in order to develop effective communication strategies to correct some of the deficits identified in this book.
- The formation of groups and branches by the political parties in communities across the island was a deliberate act to aid the process of communicating their programmes and policies to the public. The advent of electronic media, coupled with other endogenous factors such as limited financial resources on the part of the politicians, has contributed to the virtual emasculation of these groups and branches. This has negatively affected the depth of Jamaican democracy. The groups and branches were a buffer for the political parties in communities across the island, and with the rise of electronic media, they have virtually become nonexistent. A vacuum, therefore, has emerged between citizens and their leaders, and this is manifested ultimately in the apathy among voters.
- The media is now leading and shaping the political dialogue about freedom and order in Jamaica. Indeed, it has become one of the central socializing institutions in the public sphere. It uses its influence to aid

citizens in making greater political and economic choices, and this is pressuring political actors to perform or face the consequences of political and economic disaster.

- Through the expansion of the media, there has been a broadening of democratic participation in Jamaica. This has manifested itself through the talk shows that have proliferated in the country over the past twenty-five years. This proliferation has undoubtedly contributed to the greater independence of Jamaican voters. The manifestation of it is evident in the decline in grass-roots support for the major political parties and the increase in the level of listenership and viewership for various media outlets in the country. This might seem to be a paradox, but democratic participation does not confine itself to involvement with political parties. Democratic participation, according to Robert Dahl (1971), requires a consistent responsiveness to the needs of citizens. Wherever the response is seemingly positive, citizens will be receptive and participation will increase.

- In the new dispensation of political communication, political parties and their leaders have been constrained by their ability to respond to the needs of their citizens, resulting in a shift in the dependence on them. The media has thus emerged as a means by which citizens can attract attention to their needs. In the context of political communication, a theoretical argument can be extrapolated from the Jamaican experience: citizen participation and satisfaction in the democratic process depend on the nature of the political culture and the extent to which leaders communicate policy changes. If there is effective communication, participation and satisfaction will be high. Conversely, if communication is poor, participation and satisfaction will be low.

The discussion on all of these issues in this book has demonstrated that the media has had a strong effect on group membership and political party mobilization in Jamaica.

To determine the success or failure of leaders in communicating their programmes and policies to citizens of Jamaica, the structures of political communication were also examined. A systems approach was used to analyse the formal and informal institutions that exist in society to provide information and communicate with citizens. This approach recognizes the existence of the detector, selector and effector. In this analysis, the detector would be the media because it deals with the communication of information from the different structures in the society; the selector would be the cabinet because it is responsible for formulating the rules that are used to make decisions; and the effector would be the public because it deals with the transaction of information between the various systems. For the system to move towards equilibrium, that is, an efficient and effective flow of information between the governors and the governed, all the components must be operating efficiently. However, as argued and shown by the data presented here, this is not the case in Jamaica. There are gaps or breakages in the structures that have been established to facilitate the smooth flow of information among the organs of this society.

In Jamaica, the cabinet is the main decision-making body, as that is where policy is formulated and approved. However, from time to time, the cabinet has taken decisions that have frustrated citizens, many of which have been done without consulting with the people. Whenever this occurs, it leads to discontent among the citizens. But as has been lucidly articulated, that lack of consultation and dialogue with grass-roots organizations undoubtedly hinders equilibrium in the communication process. Their exclusion from the decision-making process will only serve to frustrate them, and when they are frustrated, they will abstain from the political process. This is what is being experienced in the Jamaican political process today.

Communicating with citizens is a primary requirement for the success or failure of an administration. A clear and defined strategy has to be designed to market whatever economic programmes and policies an administration seeks to implement. Using multiple sources, I examined a number of cases relating to the communication strategies of leaders in mobilizing citizens, as well as the relationship between the leaders and citizens in the participation in the political process. Seaga is seen to have suffered significantly from serious communication deficits. He had no clearly defined communication strategy, and even though he enjoyed much success in transforming the economy and generating growth in the latter half of the 1980s, these achievements never benefited the image of either him or his administration. The marketing of government programmes and policies was treated in a cavalier manner, left to the issuance of press releases and the holding of press conferences. Seaga has admitted that this was a major factor that contributed to the demise of his administration in the 1980s.

There was also a credibility factor that contributed to the varied defeats that the Seaga-led JLP suffered in the 1990s. His loan from a commercial bank that was not being serviced, and the fact that there were individuals within his own political organization that wanted to see him resign his office, created a credibility gap and contributed to the defeats in the 1990s. These issues contributed to distortions in the argumentation on freedom and order within the Jamaican society. Citizens were turned off by the message of economic management by the Seaga-led JLP, as there were too many contending issues to grapple with in that political organization. The internal strife, the departure of Golding and other important party functionaries, and the personal financial problems of Seaga all contributed to the distortion of the party's messages and to the communication problems which resulted in the defeats of the JLP until 2002.

Conversely, the Patterson administration had an effective approach to communicating to the citizens. Through the Live and Direct and Face-to-Face mechanisms, it was able to impart some of the most complex issues to the ordinary Jamaican in a comprehensible way. The administration also utilized the organizational structures of the PNP to act as a conduit for filtering its programmes and policies to its members in communities across the island. These were outside the formal communication structure that was established by the constitution – Parliament. Patterson and his administration, therefore, were able to effectively market the most complex economic programmes and policies to citizens, which contributed to the levels of success that the party enjoyed at national elections. One example was the collapse of the financial sector, a difficult economic matter to contend with, which had to be packaged and sold to citizens in the most delicate manner.

The PNP, up until the 2002 elections, was somewhat able to connect with the ongoing dialogue that was taking place on freedom versus order in the public sphere. The policies that it implemented were skewed towards enhancing the economic freedom of citizens. Whether it was the liberalization of the telecommunications sector to provide approximately 1.7 million Jamaicans with telecommunication services or the rescuing of the financial sector to protect more than one million small depositors, citizens felt that the Patterson regime had done a great deal to enhance and protect their economic freedom.

The liberalization of the economy established a market economy for the first time in Jamaica. A clear individualistic consumerist culture emerged as a result. Citizens glorified the attainment of used cars, cellular phones and other imported goods that were now at their disposal. These were economic tangibles with which they could identify, and then connect them to the campaign messages of the PNP. Also, these economic goods were in sync with the patron-clientelistic culture that existed in the society.

One of the important questions to address is whether Jamaican citizens favoured a market-driven economy. From the arguments presented here, one would readily conclude in the affirmative. However, from a political communication perspective, the answer is not as simple. A study conducted by Powell, Bourne and Waller (2007) discovered that 62.3 per cent of the respondents did not favour a market-driven economy, and only 29.8 per cent did. This seems paradoxical to the varied election outcomes of the 1990s, when the market economy was fully implemented. The PNP managed to win four consecutive elections, despite the anaemic economic growth during this period. This meant that there were other factors at play which contributed to this feat.

It is clear that any concept can be marketed once an effective communication strategy is installed, allowing even the most complicated and possibly controversial decisions to be communicated to the targeted audience. This is steeped in a capitalistic consumerist culture which recognizes the individualistic nature of humanity. This philosophy posits the view that because humans are individualistic, given the opportunity, they will be compelled to make rational choices once there is the perception that they stand to benefit.

In the context of a market economy, if there are competing forces, an individual will make a choice in favour of that which results in gaining a benefit. This reasoning is applicable to the Jamaican context of the 1990s and fits within the patron-clientelist culture described by Stone (1980).

More important, from the evidence, it seems as if the nature of the relationship between the leader and citizens has an effect on mass mobilization. If a strong relationship is established through the use of consistent communication strategies, citizens are likely to respond to their leaders – as has been demonstrated through the programmes and policies developed by political leaders and communicated to citizens in Jamaica. Patterson, for example, developed a strong relationship with the citizenry through his series of Live and Direct and Face-to-Face meetings, which assisted in promoting the programmes and policies implemented by his administration. The result was his winning three straight elections, a first for any leader in modern Jamaica.

In the lead-up to the 2002 national elections, the JLP was the political party in opposition for the longest period in Jamaica, not having tasted political victory since 1989. Obviously, something was wrong with the party's communication strategy, and this had to undergo a fundamental change. The JLP had to do something to appeal to citizens of Jamaica. A significant policy shift was needed in order for it to be seen as credible. Free education was the issue that the Seaga-led JLP turned to at this time. This issue, often associated with democratic socialism, resonated with some Jamaicans because of the experience of the Manley regime in the 1970s. Also, more Jamaicans favoured a "middle ground" approach to economic management, as was discovered by Powell and colleagues.

What the Seaga-led JLP was proposing in the 2002 elections would see the government placing education as the top priority in its socioeconomic decision-making. It also reflected a significant policy shift by the JLP, as it was under the Seaga regime of the 1980s that the payment of fees was introduced to the education system.

But while the idea of free education resonated among citizens, the Patterson-led PNP was able to secure victory, and this, it was argued, was because of three main contributing factors.

- The messenger of the "free education" concept, in the person of Seaga, was not seen as credible. The PNP marketed him as the man who dismantled the education policies of Michael Manley in the 1980s, and the man who first introduced the payment of fees for education. This helped to discredit the arguments of the Seaga-led JLP.
- There was some uncertainty among voters as to whether it was free education akin to that which had been introduced in the 1970s, or a modified policy initiative. This caused doubt in the minds of some voters.
- The PNP was able to communicate and market a number of its socio-economic achievements to the electorate in a convincing way through the issuance of a document entitled *Solid Achievements,* which listed its concrete accomplishments. The people were able to identify with the message of the PNP, as it offered tangible economic and social benefits with which they could identify.

The conclusion, therefore, is that the effective communication of social programmes to citizens is a major contributing factor to the success or failure of an administration. Voters are further stimulated when the social programme has a direct impact on them. It must be noted, however, that in the context of this analysis, the Patterson-led PNP was more successful at the polls than both the Manley-led PNP and the Seaga-led JLP during the period in question. This was because it had a more effective communication strategy for social programmes. Whether it was through the structures of the PNP, the Live and Direct initiative by Patterson or the Face-to-Face initiative by ministers and members of Parliament, the Patterson-led PNP was able to build a close relationship with citizens and was able to market its social programmes to them more effectively. The responsiveness of citizens to these communication strategies was manifested in the outcome of the elections: Patterson became the only leader in the history of Jamaica to be elected to office on three consecutive occasions.

Turning to the regional and international agendas, I again highlighted the way that a number of policies that were articulated by the leaders studied here were communicated. From the data presented, one could draw some conclusions as to the extent of the knowledge of citizens and its effect on their mobilization and participation.

The extent of the knowledge, it seemed, was heavily dependent on the degree to which a policy would give either of the political parties a competitive advantage. A party will consistently highlight a foreign or regional policy matter that it deems will be advantageous to its political survival. It will form a part of the propaganda mechanism if it stands a significant possibility of engendering a favourable election outcome.

In other words, the deliberate nature of a leader and political organization to communicate foreign policies to citizens is heavily dependent on the political advantage likely to be derived from communicating such policies. Foreign policies can be esoteric in nature. Therefore, there must be a concentrated effort for political leaders and their political parties to disaggregate the policies in understandable proportions for citizens. This is what Jamaica experienced over the period under examination.

The JLP managed to do this over the years. Its founder, Alexander Bustamante, declared from the 1960s, "We are with the West." This guided the foreign policy direction of the JLP over the years and has contributed to the political fortunes of that organization.

Conversely, the PNP, while its leaders have adopted some radical and transformative foreign policies, has not been able to "jamalize" and effectively communicate these policies. As a result, they have been unable to benefit politically. The enquiries highlighted in this book have shown that the JLP has outmanoeuvred the PNP on issues of foreign policy over the years, as the latter has not expressed its ideas in a way that effectively communicates them to citizens.

The JLP has been more successful than the PNP in dealing with its foreign policy approaches, so it has yielded greater political benefits in terms of election outcomes. This was demonstrable in the context of the Grenada invasion by the United States in 1983 and the rhetoric adopted by the Seaga regime towards communism in the 1980 election. Both instances brought political success as well as economic gains for his administration. The United States, through various donor agencies, injected significant cash into the Jamaican economy; and in the context of the supportive role played by Seaga in the Grenada invasion, the JLP and its leadership emerged victorious in the 1983 snap elections.

It was not the first time that Jamaica had seen the JLP outmanoeuvre the PNP on a major foreign affairs issue and gain political success. In the referendum of 1961, the JLP opted not to support joining the West Indies Federation because it believed that it would weaken Jamaica's quest to become a fully independent nation. The PNP was defeated in the referendum, which caused the premier, Norman Manley, to call general elections in 1962, which led to another defeat.

Communication strategies of leaders have served to engage citizen participation, and this is further consolidated by the nature of the relationship between the leaders and their citizens. The Seaga administration in the early 1980s marketed itself as the one to protect the freedom of the Jamaican citizens. It was able to communicate in a simple but effective way that it did not support communism, and with Seaga at the helm of the JLP, people were convinced, throwing their support behind that party in the 1980 and 1983 elections.

Jamaica has seen an evolution in political campaigning since 1972. It has moved from mundane street meetings to more sophisticated media campaigns. The political parties have developed different approaches towards selling their messages to Jamaican citizens. Up to the 1997 election, the Seaga-led JLP maintained a conservative approach to political campaigning, with a heavy focus on street meetings and visits to private homes.

Conversely, the Manley- and Patterson-led PNP adopted a more pragmatic style during this period, utilizing all the possible approaches to modern campaigning, as well as more conventional elements. This undoubtedly contributed to the victories of the PNP during this time. Between 1972 and 2006, the PNP won six general elections to the JLP's two.

After examining the campaign approaches of both political parties in Jamaica since 1972, I have detected five foundational factors: personality, fear-mongering in election campaigning, culture, language, and race.

Personality has played a pivotal role in the Jamaican political landscape ever since the country gained adult suffrage in 1944. Dominant personalities such as Norman Manley and Bustamante were constant staples in the body politic of the society. Citizens could be seen and heard imitating these two leaders during that era. The matter of personality took on renewed significance during the 1970s, however, when both Manley and Seaga became leaders of their political organizations. Manley was charismatic and very personable. Conversely, Seaga was more autocratic, but his personality could not be ignored. And later on, Patterson was calm, technocratic and very strategic in his thinking and action.

During the era of leadership of Manley, Seaga and Patterson, the media, particularly television, became a major source of information. Citizens could see the faces and hear the voices of their leaders on their television sets and could now identify these personalities. All three men became household names in Jamaica, and wherever they went, they drew significant public attention. Therefore, they developed an intimate relationship with the citizenry in their efforts to mobilize them to participate in politics.

Throughout Jamaica's modern political history, the factor of fear has figured prominently. In the context of the period under evaluation, this technique was seen to be prominent in the 1980 election. The Seaga-led JLP presented the argument to the Jamaican citizens that if the Manley-led PNP won the election, it would introduce communism. This perspective was based on Manley's close association with communist states such as the USSR and Cuba. Seaga knew from his study of the culture that Jamaicans placed an intrinsic value on their freedom: therefore, the perception of the introduction of communism in the island would violate and dismantle that freedom. The message was constantly repeated in advertisements and political speeches and contributed to the defeat of the Manley-led PNP.

The factor of culture has also played a dominant role in Jamaican political campaigning. *Culture* refers to the values, norms, practices and attitudes that exist within a society. In Jamaica, for example, there is a deep love for reggae and food. These two elements form a daily part of Jamaican life. Reggae, which is the dominant form of music, can be heard in every sector of the society, while there is a proliferation of food festivals across the island.

Politicians and political parties have recognized the critical nature of culture and have sought to exploit it over the years. Political rallies, street meetings and party conferences have all featured reggae music and artists as part of their agenda. Any amount of food and liquor can be had at these functions, as the parties go all out to attract votes.

Prior to 1972, folk songs could be heard at myriad political meetings across the island. In the 1972 election, the Manley-led PNP rode on a wave of popular songs that were being played at dances and on the radio stations. The adoption of these songs by the Manley-led PNP contributed to the organization's victory in 1972.

Based on the experience in the 1972 campaign and the growth of reggae in Jamaica, the Manley-led PNP introduced for the first time in the 1976 election a specific campaign song linked to the reggae rhythm. In this song, "The Message," the lyrics were specifically linked to the programmes and policies that were implemented by the Manley regime between 1972 and 1976. The song proved to be a winner, and it is still regarded by members and supporters of the PNP as one of their favourite political songs. The introduction of the campaign song in 1976 paved the way for the introduction of specific campaign songs in all subsequent elections by both political parties, as this has proven to be an effective way of communicating the programmes and policies of the political organizations to citizens.

Language plays a crucial role in any political campaign. The term refers to how people communicate with an audience orally or in print. Generally, the politician who is best able to use the language of the people is the one who is most effective in winning the support of the voters. In 1972, Michael Manley was able to capture the minds and hearts of citizens with the slogans

"Hail di Man" and "Power to the People". These words conveyed a notion of sincerity to citizens and gave them the feeling that they were really in charge. The use of these words also came within the context of citizens' experience with the Shearer-led JLP administration, with which there had been a number of conflicts during which some felt that the power of citizens was severely restricted.

In the 1980 election, the buzzwords around the campaign for the JLP were *deliverance* and *freedom*. These words came within the context of the PNP's flirtation with communist regimes and the view that Manley was going to introduce communism to the island. The Seaga-led JLP projected itself as the party that would free citizens from "political and economic bondage". The theme resonated with the electorate and contributed to the largest victory of the JLP in any election of that political party to date.

In the 1989 election, the PNP used a simple but effective set of words to form the base of their campaign: "We Put People First". This use of words came in the context of the perception that Seaga and the JLP were uncaring. Under their administration, social services experienced major cuts due to the policy prescription of the multilateral institutions, and the party was blamed for this. The Jamaican citizens thus viewed it as uncaring and voted against it in the election.

In the 2002 election, the PNP used another set of words that resonated with the voters. Recognizing the advances made with technology across the island, the PNP used the theme "Log On to Progress". In the computer revolution that was taking place in the country at the time, citizens identified with the message and gave the PNP its fourth consecutive term in office.

The final factor that has figured prominently in political campaigning in Jamaica is race, which refers to those phenotypical images that distinguish one individual from another. Jamaica has a predominantly black population, with estimates showing over 95 per cent of citizens having that pigmentation. However, since the country gained universal adult suffrage in 1944, the country has been governed by white leaders, with the exception of the period under Shearer from 1967 to 1972.

The ascension of Patterson as prime minister in 1992 started a trend of having black leaders at the helm of government. It is instructive to note that with three consecutive terms over fourteen years, Patterson has been the longest-serving prime minister of Jamaica. Stone (1973) acknowledged the fact that race plays a pivotal role in the political process of Jamaica. This is demonstrated by the fact that of the six prime ministers Jamaica has had in its history up to 2002, four were white Jamaicans while two were black, and Patterson, a black man, was the only one to be voted into office for three straight terms.

On the campaign trail, reference would be made to Patterson's race. These statements would solicit tremendous response from the audience, as it was construed as a personal contrast between Patterson and his rival, Seaga, who is a white Jamaican.

In the 1993 election campaign, Seaga made the mistake of referring to Patterson as a "black scandal-bag" ("scandal-bag" being the colloquial term for a plastic shopping bag). This reference was construed as a racial attack and caused major disquiet in the society. The statement figured prominently in advertisements by the PNP across the media and contributed to its victory in the election.

All these factors are necessary in order for one to understand and have effective communication in any democracy. They are featured prominently in the Jamaican context, and political functionaries must be cognizant of them in order to succeed in communicating with citizens.

This book has also examined new media, political communications and citizen participation. This came within the context of the period under focus, falling outside the era when new media became a dominant part of the Jamaican political landscape. The analysis was formulated to give some indication as to the difference that currently exists in terms of options for leaders to communicate with their citizens, as well as how change is effected or stymied by the media in grass-roots organizations such as groups and branches in Jamaica.

It was concluded that the discussions about the poor health of democracy in Jamaica and globally intensified during the 1990s, at about the same time that the Internet was rapidly leading a media revolution. It did not take long for many scholars and observers to connect the two phenomena in a positive way. Scholars have been optimistic that the proliferation of the media, particularly the Internet, would assist in remedying the challenges confronting democracies. The Internet has made it possible for individuals to communicate more effectively with each other through the proliferation of social media such as Twitter, Facebook and YouTube.

Governments have become a part of this development and have been setting up a plethora of social media methods to communicate with citizens. This is true of Jamaica as well, as its governments realize that if they are to curtail the growing tide of citizen apathy and frustration with the political process, new media must play a lead role. Since 2002, there has been an intensification of the effort to communicate with citizens in Jamaica via new media. However, no one can specify with any certainty the extent to which this has contributed to an improvement or decline in democracy in the country. Herein lies fertile ground for further research.

Strategic Approaches for Communicating Programmes and Policies to Citizens

Emanating from this book, a strategic approach can be formulated to the communication of programmes and policies to citizens in Jamaica by governments. It constitutes an inestimable contribution to the storehouse of knowledge, as no clear methodology had previously been established. Drawing on arguments developed by Hahn, Habermas, Dahl, Stone, Lasswell, Hall and McLuhan, lessons have been learned which would result in political leaders and their political organizations effectively communicating with citizens in Jamaica and the wider world.

The strategic approach is undergirded by the principles of participation, inclusion and strategic targeting. Citizens must be allowed to effectively participate in the public sphere and have their voices heard and acted upon. They must be included in the decision-making process and allowed to demonstrate their true potential. Their rights must be respected, and no form of discrimination must be displayed against them. The process of creating effective political communication is as follows:

1. In developing this strategic approach, the first step is to identify the audience and to determine where they would find themselves in the ongoing political communication dialogue about "freedom" and "order". So, for example, people with disabilities are vulnerable, and because of their vulnerabilities, their interests would tend to gravitate towards policies and programmes that would advance their personal development. The perspective of "order" stresses the emphasis on economic management and that there must be economic growth before any form of development can take place. The perspective also advocates that the market economy be implemented in all its forms. This would not be in the interest of people with disabilities, and hence the "freedom" perspective would be more appropriate. That perspective places greater emphasis on civil liberties and the need to place people at the centre of development.

2. The next step in the strategic approach is to formulate policies and programmes that would fit the needs of citizens. Citizens are likely to respond positively to political leaders if they take the view that their interests are being seen to by them. The formulation of programmes, policies and legislation that would address the needs of education, health, employment and access to public infrastructure is likely to bring about significant political benefit for leaders and their political organizations. The formulation of these measures must be done in consultation with

citizens, as the need for inclusivity is paramount to encouraging their participation in the political process.

3. In formulating programmes and policies for citizens, leaders must give them the opportunity to participate in forums where the decision-making is taking place. They must be included in the political parties, Parliament, statutory boards, school boards and any other such institutions that are required to make decisions that will affect them on a daily basis. This will give greater legitimacy to the messages and increase citizens' enthusiasm to participate in the political process.

4. Knowing how and where to reach these individuals is another critical step in this strategic approach. In this regard, citizens must be organized in units where they can be easily reached. These units can be in the communities or in social media, where they are able to express themselves. It has been demonstrated in this book that information flows more effectively wherever there is an organized approach to citizens in their communities, and citizens can readily identify with the source of the information and provide the requisite feedback and political benefit. Political leaders must also be aware of how to reach these individuals and to identify the varied media through which they can be reached.

5. The production of the message is also germane to this strategic approach of communicating programmes and policies of leaders and their political organizations to citizens. In this respect, those who are charged with preparing these messages must consider the peculiarities of citizens. Therefore, a profile on each target audience is necessary. Different citizens will require particular treatment in order for the message to have the desired effect. For example, due care must be given to the inclusion of sign language and closed-caption technology in the production of any message for the hearing impaired. These are visual communicators and help meet the requirement that the message be produced in accessible formats.

6. In the implementation of this strategic approach, it is also important for an avenue to be established for vetting of the production of the message by selected members of the targeted group. Those who are charged with putting out the message must ensure that the language being used is accurate and that it does not contain any offensive words. It is also important as a means of sending a signal of inclusion and participation to citizens.

7. The final step in the strategic approach is the identification of a specific reputable individual from within the different units, whether in the communities or in social media, to liaise and provide feedback to the

leaders and their political organizations. This is important to ensure that necessary adjustments may be made, depending on the response of the broader community to the message.

Political communication is a relatively modern science. Years of research has contributed to it being a more strategic and focused method of communicating government's programmes and policies to citizens. There has been a significant improvement from the old-fashioned "hit-or-miss" approach to communication. Through the utilization of work by various theorists, those who have been entrusted with the responsibility of designing messages for political leaders and organizations have the ability to launch more pointed and results-based communications campaigns. Notwithstanding this development, limited attention has been placed on the need for developing specific approaches to communicate with citizens in Jamaica. The step-by-step approach presented in this book is intended to guide those who are crafting political messages for leaders and their political organizations.

Conclusion

In this book, I have examined the subject of mediated political communication in modern Jamaica. I have advanced the argument that the success or failure of a leader and his political organization is closely linked to the effective communication strategy of programmes and policies. There are several factors that contribute to the success or failure of leaders and their political organizations, but in the context of my specific interest, and where there is a clear research deficit, I have placed a concentrated focus on the issue of political communication.

Political communication is a specific discipline that focuses on how varied political actors communicate and interact with their audiences. In the context of liberal democracy, it takes on a particular shape and form. There are two main groups in liberal democracies, liberals and conservatives. Liberals focus on issues of freedom as the means of advancing a society. Conversely, conservatives believe that order should be the fundamental priority in any development agenda (Hahn 2003). In designing messages to communicate with citizens, careful attention must be placed on these two indispensable factors by political communication specialists if political messages are to be efficaciously developed, transmitted and well received by citizens in the Caribbean.

In Jamaica, the two dominant political parties emerged from a particular political context. For centuries, the country was under British colonial rule, and as such, the political parties that were formed emerged from established relationships with the two major political parties in Britain: the Labour Party (liberals) and the Conservative Party (conservatives). The PNP has been aligned with the Labour Party while the JLP has been connected to the Conservative Party. They have anchored their programmes and policies within the context of their philosophical antecedence with the British political parties. The book has lucidly highlighted that in the context of political communication, the PNP in its policy formation embraces freedom, and the JLP promotes order.

Leaders and their political strategists have to understand the freedom-order paradigm within the context of political communication. If they are to formulate successful messages for citizens, these concepts must be understood so that they can prepare programmes and policies that will affect citizens who support these viewpoints. Message design for political parties within a modern construct cannot be left to mere chance. It has to be strategic (Habermas 1984), and as such, one must understand where the target audience falls on the political communication divide. Are they liberals or conservatives? Do they support freedom or order?

The book also highlighted the centrality of the group and branch structures to the communication strategies of leaders and their political parties. Evidently, groups and branches were formulated by the political parties in the early stages to act as a conduit to disseminate information to citizens in their communities and to provide feedback to the leaders and their political organizations. They are a pre-eminent vehicle for transmitting political messages in communities. They include media for transmitting framed messages to citizens and to get feedback for leadership action. However, over the years, the leaders and the political parties have contributed to the declination of the groups and branches and failed to properly organize them to fulfil their core mandate. The preservation of groups and branches in a modern political communication era requires hard work, as they have to compete with new and more appealing means of communication. However, these groups and branches remain relevant to the political communication process, as they are the most reliable way to transmit undiluted messages to citizens in the communities from leaders and their political organizations.

But none of the political leaders and parties have embarked on the types of reforms to capacitate the groups and branches that will allow them to function effectively in this modern political communication epoch. For example, we have not seen any leader or political party engaging in a strategic formation of groups and branches online so that political messages can be efficaciously relayed to and from them in a consistent and timely manner.

These deficiencies of leaders and their political organizations have left their communication strategies to traditional and new media. Distortions of information have emerged on a consistent basis in the society, and the groups and branches that would have been the media in the communities for the political parties are not there to debunk the misinformation. A serious communication deficit thus exists, which contributes to the high level of political apathy in the society. Urgent work needs to be done by political leaders and political parties to make the groups and branches more relevant in a modern political communication era. Work also needs to be done by members of the academic community to point leaders and political organizations towards research-driven strategies to stimulate the groups and branches in a modern construct.

In a specific way, this book has pointed to some of the approaches to political communication by three of Jamaica's leaders from 1972 to 2006. Conspicuously, we have seen that some have engaged in what Habermas (1984) refers to as "communicative action". This approach to communication requires a more consensual environment in order to be effective. In the 1970s and 1980s, this was the communication approach adopted by Michael Manley for the PNP and Seaga for the JLP. But there was never a consensus in the society for the programmes and policies that they were pursuing, as this was the era of the Cold War, in which Jamaica was deeply enmeshed. All this affected the efficacy of each party's communication strategy.

Conversely, there is what is regarded as "strategic communicative action" (Habermas 1984), which requires the approach to communication to be more strategic. In the 1990s to mid-2000s, this was the approach adopted by Patterson, and it yielded considerable political success. Patterson is the only leader in Jamaica to be elected three consecutive times, and his strategic approach was a contributing factor.

In this strategic approach to political communication, there are five major factors that leaders and their political organizations must take into consideration, especially in election campaigns: personality, culture, fearmongering, language and race. The book has shown in varied ways how these factors have played out in election campaigns and how leaders and political organizations have used them. They are sensitive issues, and when used wisely, will redound to the political success of leaders and their political organizations. More work, however, needs to be done in these areas within the context of political communication in Jamaica and the broader Caribbean.

In any scholarly work, the arguments should contribute to the advancement of epistemology. It must shed new light and perspective on the field under study. In this book, the epistemological environment has been enriched in a number of areas:

- It is the first time that any comparative analysis has been done on the communication strategies of leaders such as Michael Manley, Edward Seaga and P.J. Patterson. The book has documented, through the use of qualitative enquiries, some of the programmes and policies of these leaders and examined their communication approaches and sought to explain how the strategies contributed to their success or failure. Through the systematic approach utilized here, one can conclude that the success or failure of a leader and a political party is closely linked to an effective communication strategy for programmes and policies.
- It is the first time that any study has been done in Jamaica to evaluate the political landscape, using the concepts of freedom and order to understand the dynamics of the political environment. No previous book has sought to place the two major political parties in the perspectives of freedom and order and to explain why leaders have succeeded or failed to communicate effectively with citizens. It was highlighted in the book

that based on the varied programmes and policies enunciated by the leaders and their political organizations, the JLP is linked to order, while the PNP is linked to freedom. Powell, Bourne and Waller (2007) revealed that the majority of Jamaicans were supportive of freedom over order. This, I believe, is a major contributing factor in the electoral dominance of the PNP and its leaders between 1972 and 2006. During the period under review, there were eight national elections; the PNP won six to the JLP's two.

- Citizens are the foundation of any political process, and they have felt that they have been largely ignored when leaders and political organizations in Jamaica have sought to communicate their programmes and policies. Recognizing this situation, a strategic political communication approach has been formulated here.

If adopted and carefully implemented, this approach can contribute to the engagement of a larger segment of the population, thus increasing participation and stimulating democracy in Jamaica and the wider world.

Notwithstanding the efforts of this book, there are significant deficits in the field of political communication in Jamaica and the broader Caribbean. The book has merely scratched the surface on this subject; further work needs to be done to understand how effective communication affects the success or failure of political leaders and their ability to get citizens engaged in the political process. Urgently needed is an examination of how the new media environment is affecting the ability of leaders and their political organizations to communicate with the people. This is one of the areas for future work for me.

References

Anderson, D. 2015. "Both Political Parties Are the Same". RJR News. Podcast. 15 October. Retrieved from www.rjrnewsonline.com.

Anderson, D.M., and Cornfield, M. 2003. *The Civic Web: Online Politics and Democratic Values*. Lanham, MD: Rowman and Littlefield.

Ashby, T. 1986. "The U.S. Message to Jamaica's Seaga: It's Time to Keep Your Promise". Heritage Foundation. 2 September. Retrieved from http://www.heritage.org /americas/report/the-us-message-jamaicas-seaga-its-time-keep-your-promise.

Bernays, Edward. 1928. *Propaganda*. New York: H. Liveright.

Blumler, J.G., and M. Gurevitch. 2001. "The New Media and Our Political Communication Discontents: Democratizing Cyberspace". *Information, Communication and Society* 4 (1): 1–14.

Blumler, J.G., and D. Kavanagh. 1999. "The Third Age of Political Communications: Influences and Features". *Political Communications* 16: 209–30.

Bourne, C., and M. Attzs. 2005. "Institutions in Caribbean Economic Growth and Development". *Social and Economic Studies* 54 (3): 26–49.

Brown, A. 1998. "A Contextual Macro-Analysis of Media in the Caribbean in the 1990s". *Media Development* 45 (4): 49–54.

Buddan, R. 2007. "Voting Behaviour and Campaign Impact". *Gleaner*, 12 August. Retrieved from http://gleaner.newspaperarchives.com/.

Campbell, E. 2014. "At Least Four Election-Related Deaths in Lead-up to 2011 Poll". *Gleaner*, 16 February. Retrieved from http://gleaner.com/.

Caribbean Community (CARICOM). 2011. *A Brief History of the Caribbean Community (CARICOM)*. Retrieved from http://caricom.org/jsp/community/caricom_history.

Cerf, G.V., and E.R. Kahn. 1974. "A Protocol for Packet Network Intercommunication". *IEEE Transactions on Communications* 22 (5): 626–41.

CNN. 2001. "Bush Says It Is Time for Action". 6 November. Retrieved from http:// edition.cnn.com/2001/US/11/06/ret.bush.coalition/index.html.

Dahl, R. 1971. *Polyarchy, Participation, and Opposition*. New Haven, CT: Yale University Press.

Dahlgren, P. 2000a. "The Internet and the Democratization of Civic Culture". *Political Communication* 17:335–40.

———. 2000b. "Media, Citizens and Civic Culture". In *Mass Media and Society*, 3rd ed., edited by M. Gurevitch and J. Curran, 310–28. London: Edward Arnold.

———. 2002. "In Search of the Talkative Public: Media, Deliberative Democracy and Civic Culture". *Javnost/The Public* 9 (3): 5–26.

———. 2005. "The Internet, Public Spheres and Political Communication: Dispersion and Deliberation". *Political Communication* 22 (2): 147–62.

Dunn, H. 2005. "50 Years of Jamaica Media: Ringing in the Changes". Retrieved from http://broadcastingcommission.org/uploads/speeches_and_presentations.

———. 2011. "Caribbean Broadband and ICT Indicators". Retrieved from https://www .mona.uwi.edu/msbm/sites/default/files/msbm/uploads/Caribbean_ICT_and _Broadband_Indicators_Data_Sheet_Jamaica_2011_19-4-11.pdf.

———, ed. 2012. *Ringtones of Opportunity: Policy, Technology and Access in Caribbean Communications.* Kingston: Ian Randle.

ECJ (Electoral Commission of Jamaica). 1972. "General Election 1972". https://ecj.com .jm/election-results/general-election-1972/.

———. 1976. "General Election 1976". https://ecj.com.jm/election-results/general -election-1976/.

———. 1980. "General Election 1980". https://ecj.com.jm/election-results/general -election-1980/.

———. 1983. "General Election 1983". https://ecj.com.jm/election-results/general -election-1983/.

———. 1989. "General Election 1989". https://ecj.com.jm/election-results/general -election-1989/.

———. 1993. "General Election 1993". https://ecj.com.jm/election-results/general -election-1993/.

———. 1997. "General Election 1997". https://ecj.com.jm/election-results/general -election-1997/.

———. 2002. "General Election 2002". https://ecj.com.jm/election-results/general -election-2002/.

———. 2007. "General Election 2007". https://ecj.com.jm/election-results/general -election-2007/.

Engels, F. 2013. *The Principles of Communism.* Independent Publishing Platform.

Federal Networking Council. 1995. "Definition of 'Internet'". Retrieved from https:// www.nitrd.gov/fnc/internet_res.pdf.

Forbes, M. 2012. "Marcia Forbes: The Business of Social Media in the Caribbean". Retrieved from http://www.caribjournal.com/2012/12/27/marcia-forbes-the-business -of-social-media-in-the-caribbean/.

Franklyn, D. 2009. *Michael Manley: The Politics of Equality.* Kingston: Wilson Franklyn Barnes.

Freedom House. 2015. "Jamaica Country Report: Freedom in the World". Retrieved from http://freedomhouse.org/.

Friedman, H.S. 2012. "American Voter Turnout Lower Than Other Wealthy Countries". *Huffington Post.* 7 October. Retrieved from http://www.huffingtonpost .com/howard-steven-friedman/voter-turnout-europe-america_b_1660271.html.

Giddens, A. 1984. *The Constitution of Society: Outline of Structuration.* Cambridge: Polity Press.

———. 1991. *The Consequences of Modernity.* Cambridge: Polity Press.

Graber, D. 2011. *Media Power in Politics.* 6th ed. Washington, DC: CQ Press.

Habermas, J. 1984. *Theory of Communicative Action.* 2 vols. Cambridge: Polity Press.

———. 1989. *The Structural Transformation of the Public Sphere.* Cambridge, MA: MIT Press.

———. 1998. "Some Further Clarifications of the Concept of Communicative Rationality". In *On the Pragmatics of Communication,* edited by M. Cooke, 307–42. Cambridge, MA: MIT Press.

———. 2006. "Political Communication in Media Society: Does Democracy Still Enjoy an Epistemic Dimension? The Impact of Normative Theory on Empirical Research". *Communication Theory* 16 (4): 411–26.

Hahn, D.F. 2003. *Political Communication: Rhetoric, Government, and Citizens.* 2nd ed. State College, PA: Strata.

Hall, K.M., and M. Chuck-A-Sang. 2007. *CARICOM Single Market and Economy: Challenges, Benefits and Prospects.* Kingston: Ian Randle.

Hall, S., D. Hobson, A. Lowe and P. Willis, eds. 1973. *Culture, Media, Language.* Birmingham: Centre for Contemporary Cultural Studies.

Hallin, D., and P. Mancini. 1998. *Americanization, Globalization, Secularization: Understanding the Convergence of Media System and Political Communication in the US and Western Europe.* Boston: Cambridge University Press.

———. 2004. *Comparing Media Systems: Three Models of Media and Politics.* Cambridge: Cambridge University Press.

Hamersley, B. 2004. "Why Online Radio Is Booming". *Guardian,* 12 February. Retrieved from https://www.theguardian.com/media/2004/feb/12/broadcasting.digitalmedia.

Hill, K.A., and Hughes, J.E. 1997. "Computer-Mediated Political Communication: The Usenet and Political Communities". *Political Communication* 14 (1): 3–27.

Hobbes, Thomas. (1651) 1969. *Leviathan.* Menston, UK: Scolar Press.

Hope, D. 2013. *International Reggae: Current and Future Trends in Jamaican Popular Music.* London: Pelican.

Houses of Parliament. 2011. "Charter of Fundamental Rights and Freedoms Amendment Act". Retrieved from http://japarliament.gov.jm/.

Huntington, S.P. 1991. *The Third Wave: Democratization in the Late Twentieth Century.* Norman: University of Oklahoma Press.

International Commission for the Study of Communication Problems. 1980. "Many Voices, One World: Towards a New, More Just and More Efficient World Information and Communication Order". Retrieved from UNESCO Digital Library, https://unesdoc.unesco.org/.

Jamaica Hansard. 2002. Proceedings of the House of Representatives. Session April–July (1). Kingston.

Janda, K., and T. Colman. 1998. "Effects of Party Organisation on Performance during the 'Golden Age of Parties'". *Political Studies* 46 (3): 611–32.

Jenkins, H., and D. Thorburn. 2003. *Introduction to Democracy and New Media.* Cambridge, MA: MIT Press.

JIS (Jamaica Information Service). 2011. "New-Look JIS Website Ranks Third in Jamaica". Retrieved from https://www.jis.gov.jm.

JLP (Jamaica Labour Party). 2003. "The Constitution of the Jamaica Labour Party". Retrieved from http://jamaicalabourparty.com/.

Jones, K. 2009. *Bustamante, Notes, Quotes, Anecdotes: An Account of the Life and Times of the Right Excellent Sir Alexander Bustamante.* Self-published.

Kerr, J. 1997. *Report of the National Committee on Political Tribalism*. Kingston: Jamaica Information Service.

Kuhn, A. 1974. *The Logic of Social Systems: A Unified, Deductive, System-Based Approach to Social Science*. San Francisco: Jossey-Bass.

Lasswell, H. 1948. "The Structure and Function of Communication in Society". In *The Communication of Ideas: A Series of Addresses*, edited by L. Bryson, 117–29. New York: Institute for Religious and Social Studies.

Le Franc, E., ed. 1994. *Consequences of Structural Adjustment: A Review of the Jamaican Experience*. Kingston: Canoe Press.

Levitt, K. 1991. *The Origins and Consequences of Jamaica's Debt Crisis 1970–1990*. Mona, Jamaica: Kingston Consortium Graduate School of Sciences, University of the West Indies.

Lippmann, Walter. 1922. *Public Opinion*. New York: Harcourt, Brace.

———. 2004. *Public Opinion*. 2nd ed. Mineola, NY: Dover.

Locke, John. (1689) 1988. *Two Treatises of Government*. Edited by Peter Laslet. Cambridge: Cambridge University Press.

Manley, M. 1974. *The Politics of Change: A Jamaican Testament*. Washington, DC: Howard University Press.

———. 1978. "Address to the Special General Assembly of the United Nations". 11 October. Retrieved from http://www.anc.org.za/content/michael-manleys-address-special-meeting-general-assembly-observance-international-anti.

———. 1980. "Jamaica at the Crossroads: An Interview with Michael Manley". *Multinational Monitor* 1 (6): para 13. Retrieved from http://www.multinationalmonitor.org/hyper/issues/1980/07/interview-manley.html.

———. 1991. *The Poverty of Nations: Reflections on Underdevelopment*. London: Pluto.

Marable, M. 2007. *Race, Reform, and Rebellion: The Second Reconstruction and Beyond in Black America, 1945–2006*. 3rd ed. Jackson: University Press of Mississippi.

McCombs, M., and D. Shaw. 1972. "The Agenda-Settings of the Mass Media". *Public Opinion Quarterly* 36 (2): 176–87.

McGregor, J. 2015. "How Pope Francis Defines a Good Political Leader". *Washington Post*, 24 September, para 7. Retrieved from https://www.washingtonpost.com/news/on-leadership/wp/2015/09/24/how-pope-francis-defines-a-good-political-leader/.

McLuhan, M. 1964. *Understanding Media: The Extensions of Man*. New York: McGraw-Hill.

Meeks, B. 1991. "Remembering Michael Manley". Retrieved from https://www.solidarity-us.org/node/1991.

Mill, John Stewart. (1859) 2010. *On Liberty*. London: John W. Parker and Son, West Strand.

Ministry of Justice. 1962. "Constitution of Jamaica". Retrieved from http://moj.gov.jm/.

Ministry of Labour and Social Security. 2015. *Socio-economic Study of Persons with Disabilities in Jamaica*. Kingston: Ministry of Labour and Social Security.

Morris, F. 2001. "The Effects of Multi-Lateral Institutions on the Political Process in Jamaica". MPhil thesis, University of the West Indies, Mona, Jamaica.

Munroe, T. 1999. *Renewing Democracy into the Millennium: The Jamaica Experience in Perspective*. Kingston: University of the West Indies Press.

———. 2002. *An Introduction to Politics: Lectures for First-Year Students*. 3rd ed. Mona, Jamaica: Canoe Press.

Nagy, G.E. 2001. "Advisory Opinion No. 10-2001". In *State of New Jersey, New Jersey Campaign Financing and Lobbying Disclosure*, Election Law Enforcement Commission, 4 October. Retrieved from http://www.elec.state.nj.us/pdffiles/ao/2001/ao102001.pdf.

Nation, F. 1984. "Jamaica: Feeling the Pain of Structural Adjustment". *Multinational Monitor* 5 (7): para 5. Retrieved from http://multinationalmonitor.org/hyper/issues/1984/07/nation.html.

Norris, P. 2004. "Political Communications". Typescript. 16 February. Retrieved from http://www.hks.harvard.edu/fs/pnorris/Acrobat/Political%20Communications%20encyclopedia2.pdf.

Novendstern, M. 2011. "Facebook Democracy". *Harvard Political Review*, 8 February. Retrieved from http://harvardpolitics.com/online/hprgument-blog/communication-power/.

Obama, B. 2012. "Remarks by the President in the State of the Union Address". 24 January. Retrieved from www.whitehouse.gov/the-press-office/2012/01/24/remarks-president-state-union-address.

Padovani, C. 2008. "The New World Information and Communication Order". Retrieved from https://onlinelibrary.wiley.com/https://onlinelibrary.library.com/doi-abs-9781405186407.wbiecn013.

Panton, D. 1993. *Jamaica's Michael Manley: The Great Transformation (1972–1992)*. Kingston: LMH Publishing.

Patterson, P.J. 2018. *My Political Journey: Jamaica's Sixth Prime Minister*. Kingston: University of the West Indies Press.

PIOJ (Planning Institute of Jamaica). 1973. "Economic and Social Survey of Jamaica". Retrieved from http://www.pioj.gov.jm/.

———. 1988. "Economic and Social Survey of Jamaica". Retrieved from http://www.pioj.gov.jm/.

———. 1989. "Economic and Social Survey of Jamaica". Retrieved from http://www.pioj.gov.jm/.

———. 1993. "Economic and Social Survey of Jamaica". Retrieved from http://www.pioj.gov.jm/.

———. 2002. "Economic and Social Survey of Jamaica". Retrieved from http://www.pioj.gov.jm/.

———. 2006. "Economic and Social Survey of Jamaica". Retrieved from http://www.pioj.gov.jm/.

———. 2013. "Economic and Social Survey of Jamaica". Retrieved from http://www.pioj.gov.jm/.

PNP (People's National Party). 1978. "Principles and Objectives". Retrieved from http://www.pnp.org.jm/.

———. 2008. *The Constitution of the People's National Party*. 2nd ed. Kingston: People's National Party. Retrieved from http://www.pnp.org.jm/.

Powell, L.A., P. Bourne and L. Waller. 2007. *Probing Jamaica's Political Culture: Main Trends in the July-August 2006 Leadership Governance Survey*. Kingston: Centre for Leadership and Governance, University of the West Indies.

Press Association of Jamaica. 2018. "Press Association Calls on Government to Immediately Resume Post-Cabinet Press Briefings". 10 May. Retrieved from http://pressassociationjamaica.org/press-association-calls-on-government-to -immediately-resume-post-cabinet-press-briefings/.

Price, V., and D. Tewksbury. 1997. "News Values and Public Opinion: A Theoretical Account of Media Priming and Framing". In *Advances in Persuasion*, edited by G.A. Barrett and F.J. Boster, 173–212. Vol. 13 of *Progress in Communication Sciences*. Greenwich, CT: AbleX.

Privy Council. 2004. "Independent Jamaica Council for Human Rights (1998) Ltd. and Others v. Syringa Marshall Burnett and the Attorney General of Jamaica". Retrieved from http://iml.jou.ufl.edu/projects/spring06/watson/privycouncil.html.

Rodriquez, S.A. 1996. "The Jamaican Political Culture: A Theoretical and Empirical Exploration". MPhil thesis, University of the West Indies, Mona, Jamaica.

Rosenberg, M. 1999. "For Jamaicans, Radio Days Are Not a Thing of the Past". *Los Angeles Times*, 12 December. Retrieved from https://www.losangelestimes.com.

Schulze-Wechsungen, W. 1934. *Political Propaganda*. Translated by R. Bytwerk. Retrieved from http://www.calvin.edu/academic/cas/gpa/.

Seaga, E. 2007. "Campaign Strategy and Voting Preference". *Gleaner*, 15 July. Retrieved from http://gleaner.newspaperarchive.com/.

———. 2008. "Can We Grow What We Eat?" *Gleaner*, 4 May. Retrieved from http://gleaner.newspaperarchive.com/.

———. 2009. *My Life and Leadership*. Vol. 1, *Clash of Ideologies, 1930–1980*. London: Macmillan.

———. 2010. *My Life and Leadership*. Vol. 2, *Hard Road to Travel, 1980–2008*. London: Macmillan.

STATIN (Statistical Institute of Jamaica). 2002. "Survey of Living Conditions". Retrieved from http://statinja.gov.jm/.

———. 2006. "Survey of Living Conditions". Retrieved from http://statinja.gov.jm/.

———. 2008. "Survey of Living Conditions". Retrieved from http://statinja.gov.jm/.

———. 2011. "Census 2011". Retrieved from http://statinja.gov.jm/.

Stephens, E., and J. Stephens. 1986. *Democratic Socialism in Jamaica: The Political Movement and Social Transformation in Dependent Capitalism*. London: Macmillan.

Stone, C. 1973. *Class, Race and Political Behaviour in Urban Jamaica*. Kingston: Institute of Social and Economic Research, University of the West Indies.

———. 1980. *Democracy and Clientelism in Jamaica*. New Brunswick, NJ: Transaction.

———. 1981. "Public Opinion and the 1980 Elections in Jamaica". *Caribbean Quarterly* 27 (1): 1–19.

———. 1982. "Public Opinion Polls". *Daily Gleaner*, 27 October. Retrieved from https://newspaperarchive.com/kingston-gleaner-oct-27-1982-p-1/.

———. 1984. "Reflections on Political Polling in Jamaica". *Social and Economic Studies* 33 (1): 117–41. http://www.jstor.org/stable/27862066.

———. 1989a. "The Jamaican General Election of 1989". *Electoral Studies* 8 (2): 175–78.

———. 1989b. *Politics versus Economics: The 1989 Elections in Jamaica*. Kingston: Heinemann.

———. 1992. *Values, Norms and Personality Development in Jamaica*. Mona, Jamaica: Institute of Social and Economic Research, University of the West Indies.

Trussel, D. 2010. "'Anonymous' Captured Neda's Death and Now the Polk Award". Retrieved from https://donnatrussell.wordpress.com/2010/02/18/anonymous -captured-nedas-death-and-now-the-polk-award/.

UNDP (United Nations Development Programme). 2013. "2013 Human Development Report". Retrieved from http://hdr.undp.org/en/2013-report.

World Health Organization/World Bank. 2011. "World Report on Persons with Disabilities". Retrieved from https://who.org.

Waller, L.G. 2013. "Enhancing Political Participation in Jamaica: The Use of Facebook to "Cure" the Problem of Political Talk among the Jamaican Youth". SAGE Open. https://doi.org/10.1177/2158244013486656.

Zimbalist, A., J.H. Sherman and S. Brown. 1988. *Comparing Economic Systems: A Political Economical Approach*. New York: Harcourt College Publishers.

Index

Cuba, 35, 53, 55, 94, 95, 96, 100, 113, 114, 135, 161
culture in election campaigns, 136, 161
CVM TV, 40

Dahlgren, P., 142–43, 144
Daily Gleaner, 35–36, 114
Daily News, 35, 114
death rate, 76
democracy, 143–45; defined, 143;
economic development, 143–44;
equality, 144; foreign control, 144;
political activist, 144; subcultural
cleavage, 144; third wave of, 145
democratic socialism, 7, 26, 53, 54, 55, 88, 114, 157
detector, 43
developed countries, 93
dialogue and decision-making, 28–34
Digicel, 70
divestment of state assets, 64–65
Duncan, D.K., 116, 119
Dunn, Hopeton, 38, 147, 148–49

economic development, 143–44
economic liberalization, 7, 9, 21–22, 30–31, 37, 61, 123, 124, 144, 151, 153
economic programmes and policies, 53–74, 155–57; Agro 21 project, 63–64; democratic socialism, 53; divestment of state assets, 64–65; exchange rate, 62–63, 65–66; foreign direct investment, 60, 69; net international reserves (NIR), 60–61, 66, 69; in the 1970s, 53–55; in the 1980s, 55–57; in the 1990s, 57–61; South-South cooperation, 53; subsidies, 58, 60, 66; telecommunications, 69–70; transportation, 66–67
education, 75, 77–79
effective communication, 7–8, 13, 15–16. *See also* communication
effector, 43
election campaigns/campaigning, 105–38, 160–63, 169; culture in, 136, 161; election

of 1972, 107–9; election of 1976, 109–11; election of 1980, 111–16, *117–18*; election of 1983, 116–18, *117–18*; election of 1989, 118–23, *121–22*; election of 1993, *121–22*, 123–26; election of 1997, 126–27, *131–32*; election of 2002, 127–32, *131–32*, *133*; election of 2007, 132–34, *133*; fearmongering in, 135, 160–61; language in, 136–37, 162–63; overview, 105–7; personality in, 135, 160; race in, 137–38, 163
Employment Termination and Redundancy Act of 1974, 25
epistemological environment, 169–70
equality, 144
exchange rate, 62–63, 65–66

Facebook, 140–41
family, 24
fearmongering in election campaigns, 135, 160–61
Federal Networking Council, 139
Financial Sector Adjustment Company (FINSAC), 69
Food Stamp, 80–81
foreign control, 144
foreign direct investment, 60, 69
formal structures/institutions, 44–48; cabinets, 44–45, 155; ministries, 47–48; Parliament, 45–47
Franklyn, Delano, 94
freedom, 1–2, 14, 23, 88, 164, 167. *See also* order
freedom and order, 9, 14, 18–19, 54, 71–72, 151–52, 169–70
free education, 77–79. *See also* education

Gairy, Eric, 96
Garvey, Marcus, 91
General Agreement on Tariffs and Trade (GATT), 90
Giddens, A., 15, 18
Glasspole, Florizel, 78, 116–17
globalization, 3, 8, 31, 100, 151
Global North, 93

strategic communicative action, 169
strong communicative action, 17
structures/institutions, 43–51, 154–55;
formal, 44–48; informal, 48–51;
systems theory, 43–44
Struggle, 115
subcultural cleavage, 144
subsidies, 58, 60, 66
systems theory, 43–44; controlled system,
43; cross-sectional approach, 43;
functionalist approach, 43, 44; holist
approach, 43; reductionist approach,
43; uncontrolled system, 43

talk shows, 114
teaching of values, 22
telecommunications, liberalization of,
69–71
Telecommunications Act, 128
television, 37–38
*The Third Wave: Democratization in the
Late Twentieth Century* (Huntington),
145
third wave of democracy, 145
Thorburn, D., 142
Trades Union Congress in Britain, 24
trade unions, 24–26
training institution, 82
transaction, 43–44
transportation, 66–67
trust deficit, 3
Tufton, Christopher, 129
Twitter, 141
tyrannical rule, 14

UN General Assembly, 91–92
Union of Soviet Socialist Republics
(USSR), 53, 55, 58, 95, 96, 113, 114, 135, 161

United Kingdom (UK). *See* Britain
United Nations, 81, 91–92
United Nations Development
Programme (UNDP), 94
United Nations Education, Science and
Cultural Organization (UNESCO), 93
United States (US), 113, 116, 141, 147, 151,
152, 159; Caribbean Basin Initiative, 37;
foreign policy, 145; Grenada invasion,
79, 96–97, 116; hegemonic role, 90;
Heritage Foundation, 64; hostage crisis
in Beirut, 96; Iraq invasion, 101–3;
loans and grants from, 55; Seaga and,
55, 94, 95, 96

values, teaching of, 22
Vocational Training Centres, 82
von Bertalanffy, Ludwig, 43

Waller, L., 23, 26, 32, 33, 73, 88, 156, 157, 170
"We are with the West," 90
websites, 146–47
West Indies Federation, 90–91, 104, 159
Williams, Eric, 91
Workers Party of Jamaica, 115
World Bank, 51, 55, 56, 58, 61, 62, 63, 79,
81, 151
World Trade Centre, attack on, 101–2
World Trade Organization (WTO), 90,
100

Year of the Disabled (UN), 81
youths, skills training for, 79–80
YouTube, 141–42

ZQI, 36
Zuckerberg, Mark, 140